SHADES OF AUTUMN

Edited by

Heather Killingray

First published in Great Britain in 2004 by
ANCHOR BOOKS
Remus House,
Coltsfoot Drive,
Peterborough, PE2 9JX
Telephone (01733) 898102

All Rights Reserved

Copyright Contributors 2003

SB ISBN 1 84418 279 7

FOREWORD

Anchor Books is a small press, established in 1992, with the aim of promoting readable poetry to as wide an audience as possible.

We hope to establish an outlet for writers of poetry who may have struggled to see their work in print.

The poems presented here have been selected from many entries, and as always editing proved to be a difficult task.

I trust this selection will delight and please the authors and all those who enjoy reading poetry.

Heather Killingray
Editor

CONTENTS

Title	Author	Page
Autumnal Observations	Paul Kelly	1
Autumn	Claudia Thompson	2
A Beautiful Sight	Donald John Tye	3
Between Summer And Autumn	Kathleen M Scatchard	4
Autumn	Margaret Miles	5
Shades Of Autumn Gold	Robert Lewis	6
Farewell Summer	Robert Allen	7
Nuttal Park's Game	Robert D Shooter	8
Autumn Poet	Moira Jean Clelland	9
The Cherry Tree	Kerri Fordham	10
Summer's End	Jayne Walker	11
Autumn	Janet Robertson Jones	12
Autumn	Kay Gilbert	13
Autumn	K J Hooper	14
Leaf Fragments Blown	M C Soper	16
Autumn	J Hallifield	17
Nature's Tapestry	Dorothy Margaret Smith	18
The Right Angle	Angela Butler	19
Autumn	Gillian S Gill	20
The Gifts Of Autumn	Mary Hughes	21
Autumn Now Approaches	Kim Montia	22
Still Life	Roger Turner	23
Autumn	Christina Sturman	24
Shades Of Autumn	Irene G Corbett	25
Little Copses	Lyndsay Cox	26
Thoughts Of Autumn	Mary Lawson	27
Autumn	I Hartley	28
Autumn	Helen S Persse	30
Autumn Display	Angela Moore	31
Autumn	Joan Cashford	32
Autumn	Ruth Lydia Daly	33
Autumn Bounty	Hazel McMinn	34
Renewal	Marjorie Lloyd	36
Autumn	Ruth Daviat	37
Autumn's Chariots Of Fire	Barbara Thomas	38
Autumn Trees	Mike Monaghan	39

Autumn By Degrees	Daphne E Cornell	40
Autumn	Hilarie Grinnell	41
Autumn Glory	J Allen	42
The Autumn Light	Val Backs	43
Autumnal Glow	Tracey Lynn Birchall	44
Autumn	John Mitchell	45
Fall	Olliver Charles	46
Autumn	Joan E Milne	47
Autumn Gold	Dorothy Brooks	48
Autumn's Fate	Patricia Carter	49
Autumn Harvest	Joy Morton	50
The Season Of Change	Sheila Storr	51
The Wild Flower	Ricky N Lock	52
This Splendid Autumn Day	Margaret Doherty	53
A Beautiful Season	Glenice Siddall	54
Autumn	June M Peek	55
Autumn	Brenda King	56
Autumn	W McLean	57
Autumn	Patricia Turner	58
Autumn	David Stuart	59
Sand And Sunflowers	Rachel Mary Mills	60
Autumn/Winter	M C Jones	62
The Portrait	Irene Siviour	63
Autumn	Norma Flair Challis	64
Misty Saturday Morning	Neville Anthony	65
Autumn	M G Clements	66
Autumn	Lesley McDonagh	67
September Sisters	Linda D'Alessio	68
November Day	Norah Green	69
Autumn Leaves	G D Furse	70
Autumn Of Life	Barbara Williams	71
Autumn Leaves	Maria Ann Cahill	72
One Autumn Day	Joan Thompson	73
A Season	Julie Spackman	74
Autumn	Nicole Woollard	75
Autumn Term	Dai Blatchford	76
Autumn	Michelle Elliott	77
Season Of Silences	R N Taber	78

Autumn	Olive May McIntosh-Stedman	79
November	Chris White	80
Autumnic Sorrow	Drew Hawfawn	81
Rise	Gary Raymond	82
Autumn	Coralie Campbell	83
Glorious Autumn	George B Clarke	84
Autumn	R Vincent	85
The Mist Of This Autumn Morning	Jonathan Pegg	86
Autumn Massacre	Eifion Thomas	87
Autumn Is Here	Stacey Weeks-Pearson	88
October	Barrie Williams	89
Autumn, In An English Wood	Gordon Wilson	90
Autumn Gladness	Linda Doel	91
An Autumn Day	Geoffrey Graham	92
Another Ode To Autumn	J Morley	93
Autumn	Paul Wilkins	94
Autumn Time	Christina Gilbert	95
Autumn Is Here	Lisa Platts	96
Cider Days	Robyn Dalby-Stockwell	97
The Fruit Of Autumn	James Rasmusson	98
An Autumn Quintile	Brian Strand	99
Autumn	Alan Millard	100
September Days	Rosemary Davies	101
Autumn	Suzanne Thorne	102
Autumn	Gilly Jones-Croft	103
Autumn	E Timmins	104
Nature's Essence	Kerry Webber	105
Autumn Is Coming	Rita E Sturdy	106
The Autumn Scene	Sammy Michael Davis	107
Autumn	Jackie Sutton	108
Mother Nature's Treasure Chest	Margaret McHugh	109
Autumn On Cannock Chase	Norma Rudge	110
Our Day	Lyn Sandford	111
A Season To Treasure	Carol Bond	112
Autumn	Josepha Blay	113
Anticipating Autumn	Sandra Griesbach	114
Autumn Across The Barricades	S M Thompson	115

Our Autumn Years	Lucy Bloxham	116
Autumn Concerto	Patricia Whittle	117
Los Colores Del Otoño	Juan Pablo Jalisco	118
Autumn	Ethel Wakeford	120
Parkland King	Martyn Reed	121
Spring	Jennifer Park	122
Autumn	Diana Stannus	123
Harvest Time	Richard Unwin	124
Autumn's Tapestry	Margaret B Baguley	125
The Autumn Air	Josephine Thomas	126
Autumnal Reflections	Liam Heaney	127
Autumn Leaves	M J Banasko	128
Autumn	Pam Cole	130
Autumn	Amy Hempstead	131
Autumnal Thoughts	Sheila J Dodwell	132
Athens, Autumn	Marcia M Servente	133
Highland Autumn	Jan Ross	134
Autumn Shared	Sid 'de' Knees	135
Orientations	Michael Fenton	136
Autumn Days	G Nutbeem	138
Autumn	Jean Bagshaw	139
My Parallel Autumn	Kenneth L Tropman	140
Waspish	Dee Yates	141
Autumn	L R Jennings	142
The Leaves Start To Fall	Cynthia Scott	143
Thoughts Of Autumn	David A Garside	144
Fallen Leaves	Patricia Susan Dixon MacArthur	145
Autumn	H Leventhall	146
Autumn Jewels	Wesley Stephens	147
Instrument For War Gaming	Kelvin Carter	148
Evening Silences	Hilary Jean Clark	150
November	Christine Hardemon	151
The Drawing In	Sheila Lewis	152
November Falls	Tony Bush	153
Autumania	W Thirkettle	154
. . . Into The Wind You Go	Gemma Mountain	155
When Dancing Blaze Subsides	Henry Disney	156

Autumn's Harbinger	Barbara Robson	157
To Autumn	Janet Cavill	158
Autumn	Dorothy Squires	159
Autumn Leaves	F R Smith	160
Autumn's Past	C E Growcott	161
Cessation	Sarah Blackmore	162
Autumn	Brenda Lismer	163
Autumn . . .	Ceejay	164
Autumn	J P Worthy	166
Autumn	Phyllis O'Connell	167
Autumn Blues	Ken Rolfe	168
September's Legacy	Kinsman Clive	169
A Poem For Autumn	Sandra Benson	170
Shades Of Autumn	Carole Harradence	171
Autumn Leaves	Lorna June Burdon	172
Autumn Time	A F Hiscocks	173
Elements	Laurent Rickling	174
It's Autumn-Atic!	Denis Martindale	175
Mixed Feelings	Cathy Mearman	176
Autumn	Sheun Oshinbolu	177
Five More Minutes	Nikki Healey	178
SAD	Naomi Donegan	179
Mother Nature	Jorunn Ingebrigtsen	180
Different Colours	George Reed	181
Autumn	Marjorie Ridley	182
Autumn Time	H H Steventon	183
Autumn . . . Is It Good Or Bad?	Mrinalini Dey	184
A Touch Of Frost In The Autumn Air	Norman Bissett	185
Pictures In The Fire	Liz Osmond	186
Tywardeath	Vann Scytere	187
Autumn's Glory	Dan Pugh	188
Autumn Festival	Celia G Thomas	189
The Silent Still	Gina Bowman	190
A Reason To Cuddle	M N Darvil	192
Autumn Harvest	Andrew Farmer	193
The Soft Contented Sigh Of An Autumn Breeze	Brian L Porter	194

Autumn Days	Patrick Davies	195
The First Of Fall	Margery Rayson	196
Autumn	Derek Spencer	197
Autumn	Jessie E Bishop	198
Autumn Returns	Beth Izatt Anderson	199
Where Silver Spider Webs And Frost Covered Blackberries . . .	Jackie J Docherty	200
The Fox's Point Of View	Jane Margaret Isaac	202
Autumn	Barbara Ann Barker	203
A Time To Rest	Judy Taylor	204
Autumn's Magical Mile	S M Bush-Payne	205

AUTUMNAL OBSERVATIONS

Golden leaves wither,
crisply past their prime.
Some hover painfully,
prolonging the agony,
hopeful of avoiding the drop.
Others swirl skywards,
frenetically craving attention,
bending to the dictates of the wind.

The rest linger,
dodging our footsteps,
squelching for mercy,
pleading for a second chance.
Blithely we ignore them,
crunching each carcass with relish.
Kicking their corpses,
triumphantly through the air.

Paul Kelly

Autumn

Mist on the marshes, dew on the ground,
Watery sun with a chilliness around
Days become shorter, evenings long and dark,
The developing season is making its mark.

Autumn: the time when conkers fall,
Apples are gathered for the harvest stall,
Hallowe'en pumpkins in candlelight,
Sparkling fireworks on a starry night.

Green transforms to colours so bold,
Shades of red, brown and gold,
Maturing leaves swirl silently down,
Coating paths in country and town.

Hedgehogs search for a cosy bed,
To sleep throughout the months ahead,
Migrating birds flock together,
Ready to travel to warmer weather.

Bonfires crackle in the open air,
Blackberries ripen everywhere,
Gardens shelter fading flowers,
Seeds dispersed by wind and showers.

Autumn: the season of alluring ways,
As nature prepares for colder days,
Magical hues bring a radiant glow,
A transition through to winter snow.

Claudia Thompson

A Beautiful Sight

As I sit and watch
The autumn sun
Slowly setting below
The far-off horizon
What a beautiful sight it looked

I then sat and watched
The bright autumn moon and stars
Slowly rising high
Into the cloudless autumn sky
And that was also a beautiful sight
And both of those beautiful sights
Remind me of a woman
A very sweet and beautiful woman
Whose name was Yvonne Burnip

But now I'm old and grey
And no longer do I know
Where that angel now lives
And so I won't be able to thank her
For all the love and friendship
That she gave to me
When we were both young and carefree.

Donald John Tye

BETWEEN SUMMER AND AUTUMN

Green hills rising,
Where distant sheep,
Small as white bumble bees,
Move on the grass.

Shadows cloud cast,
Give chase, extend,
Blend into evening,
Gradually.

Nights drawing in,
Late summer days,
Precious and inviting,
While autumn waits.

To change the scene,
Inside fur coats,
Small caterpillars curl,
To be transformed.

September dawns,
Half in summer yet,
A harvest yield from field,
Lane, tree and sea.

Between the trees,
Pale amber light,
Then night, with melon moon,
Large, autumn ripe.

Kathleen M Scatchard

AUTUMN

Dusk - autumn.
In the east, the sky steel grey.
In the street
bright lamplight falls on the leaves of trees
shining brilliant
gold and bronze.
The western sky opalescent
but with blazing brilliant clouds,
and Venus and a silver sickle moon.

Margaret Miles

SHADES OF AUTUMN GOLD

Rolling fields, forest in breeze
Monuments tall, beautiful trees
Leafy branches, once overflowing
Summer colours, now slowly going

Whistling wind, through tree top
Leaves of summer, start to drop
Tinted green, falling to ground
Gently floating, making no sound

Trees uncovered, in impending cold
With summer passing, autumn unfolds
Branches bare, woods once dark
All can be seen, is naked bark

Woodlands, once green and lush
Now silence throughout, deathly hush
Leaves give pleasure, to behold
Shades of yellow, autumn gold

Back to earth, whence they came
Forests wait, for life again
Birds long gone, trees forlorn
Awaiting spring, again reborn.

Robert Lewis

FAREWELL SUMMER

Summer fades away, now sad autumn's gain
with fretful, insistent rain upon the windowpane.
The geranium stands upright and proud,
solitary now where once was a crowd.

Clasping dead skirts about her
she clings to the dying warmth of summer.
Fearful of the fading light
as an ailing man of the night.

The geranium's companions once green
no longer the colour they had been.
Pale now in cold autumn's sun.
Wrinkled and brown now life is done.

Robert Allen

Nuttal Park's Game

Football match
weather crisper
in Nuttal Park Ramsbottom
near the River Irwell

took me back four decades
to when I played in such team sports
for school
and youth club
for fun.

Everyone hoping someone else still had energy
or talent
or ideas
now that the starting joy had faded
and the finishing whistle endless in coming.

Had forgotten the agony of the end
waiting for it
then and now.

Robert D Shooter

AUTUMN POET

I jumped out into the street
The angry winds whipped up the leaves
And my skirts
Suggesting it were autumn
My hair immediately wrapping
Itself around my face

After starring at a thousand books
Containing a million words
I had remained unsympathetically
Word baron all morning

The cruel weather today was unkind to me
It had no morals
Stealing my papers and transporting them
Outwards and upward to the heavens

The poet whose audience was expressionless
Had a rush of thoughts
And returned and sat down
With pen in hand and scribbled
On the back of an old programme
Of no importance to myself.

Moira Jean Clelland

THE CHERRY TREE

A cherry tree stands blighted,
Its fruits are barely formed,
Dripping, mildew, sour berries,
Hoards of insects swarm
The sticky, ailing boughs,
Rotten to the core,
Sweet fruits born there once,
Won't blossom anymore.

Kerri Fordham

SUMMER'S END

The summer sun has all but perished
As the long nights draw in
The golden leaves fall from the trees
Like kites caught up in the wind

The rain now beats down from above
While the ground is sodden under foot
And soon we'll be greeting the ice and frost
With memories of the summer lost

The garden's now quiet from the lark's pretty song
Due south I think they have all gone
Not many creatures seem to scurry or creep
As the earthbound beasts enter their deep sleep

Storms now greet us like a long lost friend
And the dark cold winter engulfs the summer's end
Our thoughts now turn to bonfires and Hallowe'en
Soon to be replaced by Christmas's imminent return.

Jayne Walker

Autumn

The beauty of the forest trees
Where leaves have turned to gold
Would that ageing be so gentle
As we ourselves grow old
Each leaf that falls upon the dew
Was once coloured a different hue
That leafy green just turning red
Lies crumpled now on rustic bed.
God's earth is completely covered
With a carpeting of leaves
That have fallen gently
From those majestic trees
And as you trample through them
Crunching leaves beneath your feet
Lift your face up to the sky
As though your Saviour you would meet
In that glorious open space
Of cloud and sun and sky
Praise Him with your heart and soul
And sing His name on high.

Janet Robertson Jones

AUTUMN

I love autumn, a season of delight,
There is so much colour and change.
The leaves turn golden and berries are bright,
Altogether a most charming range.

I know one is sorry to see the summer pass,
But autumn is more settled and serene.
There may be a heavy dew on the grass,
Which just adds to the beauty of the scene.

September and October are good months of the year,
Much fruit and other produce do they yield.
The winter migrants shortly will appear,
And what joy it is to walk in wood and field.

At night we see the lovely Harvest moon,
So large and golden in the evening sky.
And though the winter will be coming soon,
Enjoy the autumn now, for it will quickly fly.

Kay Gilbert

AUTUMN

Delicate, dusted pink blossom, berries; black, red, with sloe, haw and dog rose, hip, dress the bramble-lined hedges with their seasonal fruit. Rolled up carpets of spring, summer growth stacked and stored as winter feed. Elongated shadows animated, still; tractors crisscrossing fields, like fishing boats, draw flocks of feeding seagulls in their wake; harrowed, ploughed the soil lies naked, exposed; as spiders, in meadows, spin their webs into a glistening sea.

Housemartins and swallows, white and black flecks, fill the early September skies; tumbling, falling, skimming water and grass, portents of the wind-blown leaves. Farms aglow with cowshed lights, country lanes and urban roads transformed, in brief, to newborn streams. The trailing hem of winter's coat, the cold embrace of morning air. In woods, copses, individual trees, flickering embers scorch the edges of leaves; the rising temper of the awakened wind fans the flames of seasonal fire.

The first touch of the rising sun, unveils, beneath the fading moon, a portrait; a landscape of shade and light. Fragrant smoke drifts, languidly, skyward, from the burial mounds of garden waste. Drainage ditches filled with rain; worn arboreal robes transformed by the Midas touch of dawn and dusk. The clocks go forward, daylight retreats; bursts of colour, flowering, blossoming; the promise of spring in the garden of the night.

Flights of starlings, synchronised, symmetrical, twist and turn, weaving their intricate patterns; the sombre plumage of rook and crow is, for an instant, clothed in gleaming light. The roe deer puts on its dark brown coat. Sycamore, beech, horse chestnut and oak harness the wind to sow their seed. Migrating birds arrive, depart. Hedgehogs, in beds of wood and leaf, embark upon their torpid sleep.

Swirling, tumbling, falling, gleaned from the loose held grip of sapless branches; leaves, in a graceful, yet sorrowful dance; whose steps and movements are set to the music of the wind, descend to the ground, and settle with a sigh. In parks, lanes, and tree-lined streets, meandering children, to the sound of retreating waves on a pebble strewn beach, wade, with shuffling steps, through the drifts of leaves. Gathered together by the sweeping hand of the wind; lifeless, dry, the shed garments of the mourning trees.

K J Hooper

LEAF FRAGMENTS BLOWN

Wind below the mountain top, blows on secret ways
Flows here obsessively through the sky,
Flows quietly into the sunlight guided by 'laws',
Incandescent motes, and tiny particles lit
Here below the mountain and above the houses of the village.
Wind below the mountain top blows on secret ways.

M C Soper

AUTUMN

Autumn is a time of maturity,
Preparing for the next season to be.
Fruit is ripe upon the tree,
Ready to be gathered by you and me!
Leaves are changing colour and ready to fall,
Creatures ready to hibernate away from it all!
Nature is getting ready to take a rest,
Nights drawing in at Earth's request.
There is still some sun at this time,
Which is more mellow like gold with less shine!
There is a chill in the night air,
Out comes the warmer clothes to wear!
Autumn is a special season,
It comes with nature's clime and reason.
Nice to have changes in our year,
God's gifts which we should hold dear.
Autumn is special so enjoy this time,
A good taste of mellow matured wine.
It is about organising and preparation,
Ready for winter coming in our direction.

J Hallifield

NATURE'S TAPESTRY

Glorious autumn, nature's showcase
Bathed in colour
Ere cold winter shows his face
Trees aglow
Bronze, russet, gold
Such a scene, so bright, so bold
Jewelled berries in abundance -
Ruby drops on rowan borne
Orange-bright on firethorn
Luscious red virginia creeper
Covering barn and hiding wall
Revel in this tapestry
Nature's art surpasses all!

Chillier nights bring morning mist
Lawns with diamond dewdrops kissed
Crystalled cobwebs grace the hedgerows
Sparkling in the rising sun
Revel in this tapestry
This show is free
For everyone.

Dorothy Margaret Smith

THE RIGHT ANGLE

There's an obliqueness about autumn
that reduces the angle of perception
and gives more than it takes away;

spring scrambles vertically green upon green,
summer jostles for space horizontally
outcolouring colour in field and garden
along lane and river bank, exploiting
the energy of the pliant earth;

slowly the sun casts longer shadows
calls to a reckoning all things green
and russet tints red to subtler yellow
sear the conscience with a sense of loss;

a thin wind scatters the leaves, the stubble
is all that is left of the golden days
but the seed offers the ransom
and pays the price the earth requires.

Angela Butler

AUTUMN

The heat of the sun is weakening,
The sun is now moving away,
Some leaves on the trees are dying,
Which signifies winter is on its way.

Early mornings are very chilly,
The same can be said of the nights too,
During the days the warmth is comfortable,
So it's a lot easier to do the things you have to do.

Some leaves are starting to change colour,
The grass isn't growing so fast,
After the grass and the hedges are cut next time,
It should be a cut that will last.

The things that sadden me about autumn,
Is losing the beauty of the flowers that adorn my days,
I'll also miss all the wild birds in my garden,
As for winter most fly away.

The nights aren't as light as they were,
Soon there will be more darkness hours,
Our windows will now have to start closing,
As the winds start to show us their powers.

We have only moved into autumn,
It's a pleasant time of the year,
The weather's a lot easier to cope with,
But sadly it's a time when our beautiful gardens start to disappear.

Soon smoke will be billowing from my neighbour's chimney,
Our gardens will be quiet and still at last,
We'll have to sort out our warm woolly jumpers,
As that nice warm sun will be a thing of the past.

Gillian S Gill

THE GIFTS OF AUTUMN

Reluctant gold is clinging to the trees,
Weeping at parting from the darkening eves,
Comforting evergreens cling here and there,
True loyal friends when winter appears.

As eyes see the beauty of burnishing gold,
Our hearts become filled with a treasure untold.
For the warm golden harvest is blessing our days,
With the warmth of His heart in spite of our ways.

Remember these days and their gifts all of gold,
As sunlit the treasures of autumn unfold,
To store in the memory against that far day,
When cold winds will herald that snow's on the way.

Mary Hughes

Autumn Now Approaches

Autumn now approaches
Trees will drop their leaves aflame
Spreading warmth with foliage
Of burnished red acclaim

Heaps of gold and copper
Soon will gather in the breeze
They'll tremble with excitement
As the season's fingers tease

Shiny, rich brown conkers too
Will bounce upon the ground
Then nestle in amongst the grass
Just waiting to be found

Temperatures will fall
And rain will puddle up the earth
Howling winds will serenade
The trees who sway with mirth.

Kim Montia

STILL LIFE

Warm, peaceful evening,
Soft lamplight of pale gold,
An autumn fire smoulders
And sweet-scented pine logs hiss.

Calm upon a polished table
Fall petals of late flowers,
Bronze-gold, blood-russet, white:

And quietly into lone corners
Seeps the slow tide of gradual darkness.

Outside an echoless dream-sky of ebony,
Trees of stifled gloom,
Lace-leafed, unstirring boughs.

In his soft-feathered flight an owl
Shrieks
In the night's deep stillness.

Roger Turner

AUTUMN

Autumn is a time of rest,
God in His wisdom knows what is best.
    Autumn is a time for sleeping,
    Waiting for winter to come creeping.
All the bright flowers start to fade,
The trees shed their leaves there will be no shade.
The sun loses its power, the days grow colder,
The daylight is shorter, the nights get bolder.
    Everything must have a time to sleep,
    A time to laugh, a time to weep.
We must have the dark to appreciate light,
We have to have wrong to know what is right.
    Autumnal colours are beautiful but sad,
    Thoughts turn to the summer that we have just had.
We long for the warmth, we long for the light,
We want everything to be always bright.
    But here in the real world this cannot be,
    We have to be caged before being set free.
This is what autumn is for
Making things sleep, this is God's law.
    But when the resting time is through
    Autumn and wintertime too.
    Then spring comes again so fresh and new
    Ready for summer and lots of things to do.
Autumn then comes round once more
The circle is complete, this is what living is for.

Christina Sturman

SHADES OF AUTUMN

Orange, red, gold and brown
Shades of autumn cover the ground
As an artist brush and palette
The countryside is touched
So God touches, each tiny leaf
As country lane, and city square
Are transformed, beyond compare
Autumn sunshine, colours our world
As floating leaves, downward are hurled
Green of summer fades away
As colours of gold, brighten our day
Too soon the skies, will turn to grey
As days grow shorter, in every way
Dark days of winter, on us descend
Birds fly, to and fro
Swallows, to foreign climes
For warmth, do go
Robin to our gardens return
To meet the winter blow
In this world, of trouble and strife
Brings joy, and hope, into our life
Changes, God seasons of nature
From green, to gold, to white
He'll turn our world and make it right
As shades of autumn
    Make it bright.

Irene G Corbett

LITTLE COPSES

Autumn.
The season, as quick
as my eye. I travelled swiftly
hedges speeding by. Deep
blue sky and floating clouds
shroud little copses in a
morning lullaby. Miles and
miles of telegraph poles running
like stitches through fields unfold.
Joining ploughed, brown with bronze
and shimmering gold. The sun slipped
behind a cloud, unseen, and
very proud of its freshly
painted autumn scene.

Lyndsay Cox

THOUGHTS OF AUTUMN

After a very hot summer,
Thoughts of autumn to me,
Do occur of that I agree,
When summer finds me all at sea.

Autumn is a time of tranquillity,
No mad rush to beat the weather,
Time now to enjoy all your endeavours,
Before winter hits you sideways.

The skies are purest blue,
With white fluffy clouds sailing through,
It is an artist's dream come true,
The ever changing view is fleeting.

So, catch it when you can,
Gardens are full of colour too,
The sun does not beat down so harshly,
Nor do thoughts abound so rashly.

Just take a walk on the wild side,
The green of the grass is luscious and deep,
The rowans on the tree sit with much pride,
Berries of the holly take autumn in their stride.

Other trees shine out over the countryside too,
Their autumnal hues attack the senses,
When green leaves turn to yellow before dropping off,
The fiery red of maples, one must see.

Everywhere you go there is something to admire,
Elderberry trees flourish, the chestnuts are ready,
There is nothing better than battling the breezes,
So, autumn is a time to relax and feel at ease.

Mary Lawson

AUTUMN

Beautiful trees gold, russet and brown
They stand in all their glory.
As the mellow sun shines through
In a sky of azure blue
In England now.

Autumn is a wonderful season
Nature has done so well
Now she stands in all her glory
What a story she can tell
Blackberries on the bushes are black and ripe
The farmer stands near the gate
Smoking his pipe
Watching birds flying overhead
Their wings wheeling, ever wheeling
One can hear their plaintive cry.

Plough shears turning rich brown earth
Big 'Boxer' and 'Darkie' straining at the girth
The golden stubble where not so long ago
Golden corn stood swaying to and fro.
In England now.

Come golden autumn, come to see what is in store
Big, juicy blackberries hang in great clusters galore
Apple, pears, plums, damsons so blue
Hazelnuts on their branches so true
All of these things and many, many more
Lady autumn agrees with her sunny smile
Yes! All is well, she says after a while
She will hand over to winter
Her turn will surely come
With cold east winds, vast snow storms,
Everything will be cold and stark.

Days and nights seem forever dark
But really the things that nature holds so rare
Are sleeping, resting, waiting to compare
With the seasons as everyone surely knows
Will continue to come as each year grows.

I Hartley

Autumn

Autumn . . . a time for reflection
On days gone by of such perfection.
The rich bounty of summer
Begins to fade away.
Migrant birds no longer stay . . .
Flying to warmer lands.

Many leaves change their colour
As the sap begins to ebb.
Silver threads of a spider's web
Form on plants and bushes.
Squirrels scamper here and there
Seeking nuts for their winter fare.

Robins chirp and hop around
Looking for grubs in the ground.
Singing their plaintiff song.
The taste of wild blackberries
Still hanging on the bushes.
The smell of bonfires at dusk.

Beautiful skies and sunsets.
All these are joys of autumn.
Seasons pass through storm and strife.
Such is the pattern of life.
The power and might of nature
Is eternal throughout the world.

Helen S Persse

AUTUMN DISPLAY

Tall, spreading, swaying, rain soaked, heavy laden trees
Full of fading, sad, reluctant, multi farious leaves
Displaying hues of golden, ochre, russet, chestnut and chocolate brown
Meekly awaiting mighty gusts to force, flutter and tumble them down.

Bushes and hedgerows bursting with ripe nutritious
   Delicious, red and blackberries
An attractive feast, beckoning hungry wild birds
   Even little fairies
Tempting rosy-red apples, green-gage
   And deep damson plums ready to go
Into safe, sturdy wicker baskets
   Before strong north winds blow.

Bright blue summer skies
   Now a soft azure grey haze
Bewitched by autumn's alluring
   Appealing misty gaze
Hills and valleys once fertile
   Bustling green and lush
Perfectly poised, gently singing
   Humming and whispering hush

Busy swallows preparing for migration
   To a faraway sunny place
Shining silver salmon leap
   Then retreat to join nature's autumnal race
Strawberry blonde cornfields smile a golden goodbye
   Whilst dancing in the breeze
Hay stacked high, land in repose
   Soon to recover after winter's deep freeze.

Angela Moore

Autumn

I love the warm, golden mornings in autumn
The marigold draped with dewy web
The michaelmas daisies with bright eyes shining
And the overwhelming painful beauty
Makes you wish you were dead.

Single asters turned upwards to golden sky
Gentle mists float over trees and lawn
And quiet blackbirds turn dry leaves where insects lie
Silent fluffy sparrows work intently on the bough
And late young ones yawn.

Joan Cashford

AUTUMN

The trees look so glorious,
Sunshine shimmers a halo around,
While falling leaves echo
Crisp, crunch, on the ground.

The leaves are all colours,
Red, copper and gold.
Some leaves are much duller
As they are quite old.

Misty, mellow mornings,
Brisk walks in afternoons,
The shadows of the evening fall,
Soon birds sing a night-time tune.

The sharp, cold winds are coming
As harsh winter draws nigh
So 'say goodbye to autumn'
Hear the swaying trees sigh.

'We were beautiful a little while
Now bare branches stretch up high,
Still, next year, glorious once again,
We'll dazzle the autumn sky'!

Ruth Lydia Daly

Autumn Bounty

The swallows gone,
So welcome when in April they returned,
The crows with saddest call,
Remind us daily that the summer's o'er,
And we are slipping into 'fall'.

Can it be true?
These glorious, sunny summer days all over,
We so enjoyed their happy carefree hours,
But let us not be sad,
For autumn offers richest stores.

Her stores most rich,
Just bursting at the seams with treasures,
The rarest gilts and bronze and golds,
No better found in earthly mines,
Such wealth and bounty holds.

What glorious fruits,
Blackberries staining our hands and lips,
As we gather freely from the hedgerows,
We must be quick,
For soon they'll be sweet pickings for the crows.

And ruby plums,
And apples sour and sweet compete,
To win attention, as at our feet they fall,
Such wondrous flavours eaten fresh or baked or jellied,
These timeless treats fill baskets in the hall.

And from the ground,
Our basic wholesome foods are reaped with joy,
Potatoes, barley, wheat and vegetables galore,
Yield to our gentle gathering,
And fill our winter store.

The seasons change,
Blest providence ensures it must be so,
So whether it be winter, spring, sweet summer or the 'fall',
Each with your different and peculiar pleasures,
We welcome you, we love you all.

Hazel McMinn

RENEWAL

Autumn's colouring hand withdraws
The scene is set for fall and fade
Summer's habit lies in tatters
Her garment green is all unmade.

The broken leaf, the soil's new guest,
Assumes its ordered passage to its transmutation
By diverse means and unseen hands
Its parts new-joined for future recreation.

Then clad in flesh or wingéd coat
The long year's wisdom seeks the earth
Midst change and chance, and wind and weather
The germ of life awaits rebirth.

And more, the myriad branch tips
Whilst they seem undressed
Reveal close-guarded buds
In patient symmetry compressed.

The circling thread will hold us fast
Can there be death or loss or even sorrow?
The old, the young, the wise endure
This threefold hope ensures tomorrow.

Marjorie Lloyd

Autumn

The scene is set, September mould
monopolises centre stage,
sensations hint at regal gold,
a precious year's advancing age.
Blue mists, like unshed tears, suggest
a turning point, the need for care,
spiralling dreams are laid to rest
and resignation brought to bear;
leaves whisper of a world beyond,
its seniority benign,
autumn and Heaven share a bond,
age's influential sign,
paint antiquity with madder,
the bronzed horizons rose-hue-topped,
retrospection makes hearts gladder,
timorousness of passing stopped;
reveries revel in design,
candelabra-like, semi-nude
extremities of arbour line
comprise distinguished interlude.
The dowager deep cherry sun
persists and cherubim intone,
embracing sky when day is done
and glowing autumn lets alone
anticlimactic residue,
the vestiges of summer spree,
appeasement couched in saffron hue
and ruby's red profundity.

Ruth Daviat

AUTUMN'S CHARIOTS OF FIRE

The north wind's unleashed the chestnut steeds
which hurl the golden chariot away
flinging the russet leaves aloft
with hooves which spark the fire of day.
The whirling whip urges the stallions on,
tossed tails and manes go swirling higher
hurtling across the forest paths
the chariot strikes the flint of fire.
Racing across September's ruddy gold
the stallions seek October's crimson blaze
firing the summer to a scarlet tint
so all the land glows in a rosy haze
vermilion and orange and ochre and yellow
the spinning wheels reap the wild willow.

Then south the north wind turns the horses' heads
seeking the lazy summer valleys green
snorting and blowing frosty air they come
showering ice crystals where summertime was seen.

When the land is ablaze the horses' tails
droop by the chariot wheels;
their work is done and back to the stalls
silently they steal.

All the world wakes and autumn is lost
the splendour is covered and white with hoar frost.

Barbara Thomas

AUTUMN TREES

Autumn trees
Are sad trees
In melancholy cloaked
In requiem saluting
A summer gone.

Red and russet
Paper-light
Falling . . .
Leaf moulders
Chestnut hunters
Treading . . .
Damp decay
Under a strained sun.

I mourn
With autumn trees
Misted and rimed
With desperate hands
Embalmed in an underworld.

Mike Monaghan

Autumn By Degrees

As the sun guilds the rooftops' golden brown
and the crisp, bright morning silvers the ground
we know autumn's here with its amber hue
for the nip in the air makes life feel new
summer's behind us for another year
with its sultry heat and stifling air
now Christmas is just weeks away
and fresh expectations fill each day
there are cosy fires with crackling wood
that makes the autumn feel so good
the crunchy leaves fall from the trees
as life cools down by a few degrees
to prepare us all for winter's cold
as this year grows steadily old
so it's time to enjoy for another year
the splendour of autumn now it's here.

Daphne E Cornell

AUTUMN

Where have the green trees and plants of summer gone?
Over the winds and breezes blow the last hot days.
The season is changing from one to one,
And everything seems out of phase.

Last summer's heat is dwindling now,
And insects and bees are still in flight.
In a hurry they are, in a frenzy they are,
Before the last pollen has lost its memorable sight.

Bright yellow is the grass, from too much sun,
Parched without rain, the ground is cracked and dry.
Swallows flying to another warm climate, seem on the run -
All the trees have lost their leaves prematurely, falling from the sky.

At last, the cooler breezes blow the hair,
And sudden gusts cause fallen leaves to whirl.
Colder nights and mornings bring the frosts, without a care.
September brings a start to autumn, to summer fond farewell.

Autumn, with its gold and rusty yellows,
Its beauty is renowned.
For every shade of coloured leaf and flower,
Turns the season into Heaven bound.

Hilarie Grinnell

Autumn Glory

Seasons come and seasons go,
You have to go with the flow.
End of summer can be sad,
But looking forward can make you glad.

There's a different feel in the air.
The wind blows softly through your hair,
Slightly chilly on your face,
You start to slow down your pace.

Green leaves turning gold, brown and red,
Such vibrant colours that turn your head.
Some birds take flight and suddenly go,
To a warmer place before the snow.

We start to put our heating on,
Nights pull in, there's less warmth in the sun.
But autumn has its own glory,
Look around and read its story.

There are seasons in our life,
Of joy, peace, stillness and strife.
But there's always treasures to be found,
As animals burrow underneath the ground.

Conkers on trees all shiny and brown,
Like folk all dressed to go to town.
Our summer tan has started to fade,
But that shouldn't make us at all afraid.

Embrace this autumn in your soul,
The stillness and God can make you whole.
And soon winter will appear,
Then after that it's another year.

J Allen

THE AUTUMN LIGHT

The autumn light it filters through
it promises love for me and you.
The love that is God's - filters through -
see it and grasp it - it will make your life new.
Born you will be when you open your heart
let your soul sigh . . .
O Lord fill my heart - with your wonderful light
which is beauty and love - as I see it
filter through from above . . .
O wonderful light - O wonderful love
as I see the autumn light
shine out . . . with your love
Shine on me - make my heart new
fill it O saviour only with you.
For my heart now calls
I only love you . . .
as I see the autumn light
filter through.

Val Backs

AUTUMNAL GLOW

Last marigolds shine brightly
but brittle leaves tinged red and gold,
tell summer's all but gone now
as autumn takes firm hold.

Mischievous winds whip through branches,
swirling leaves to greater height,
through crevices comes whistling
then frosts begin to bite.

Now deeper layers of rustling leaves
in hues of rusty brown,
crunch underfoot as squirrels chase
and nuts thud to the ground.

Dusk falls early this time of year
with a chill as midnight chimes,
soon branches bare will silhouette
landscapes of wintertimes.

Tracey Lynn Birchall

AUTUMN

The energy of summer now slowly ebbs,
With chilly mornings and dew on the webs.
The fruits of nature have reached their best,
Harvest is complete, and now there's quiet rest.

Golden stubble turns brown 'neath the plough,
And fruit are gathered from off the bending bough.
Barns and larders crammed till they overspill,
Fuel is stored to fight off the winter's chill.

The leaves have gone from the elm and oak,
Their limbs engulfed in autumn's foggy cloak.
An eerie silence spreads across all creation,
While, nature sleeps in suspended animation.

John Mitchell

FALL

Morning comes and calls me to the window -
Nature is waking from her bed of leaves.
Apples and pears dotted around the lawn,
Like balls scattered on a snooker table.
The leaves are changing to a mottled brown,
Lucky ones patterned like butterfly wings.
The fashions change to follow the season,
As the primary colours fade away.
Sign of the times, a horizon of cranes -
Those mechanical trees that bear no fruit.
There's something different about twilight
Falling on the chess pieces made of wood.
We'll soon cheat time by turning back the clock,
But still the leaves will continue to fall.
Calmness descends with the darkening sky,
As nature and children call it a day.
Another ripe apple thumps on the ground,
Whilst another shy leaf silently falls.

Olliver Charles

Autumn

The leaves are turning red and gold,
A lovely picture to behold.
They're interspersed with evergreen,
The prettiest sight you've ever seen.
The birds are picking berries bright,
And soon the swallows will take flight.
The harvest has been gathered in,
And now the nights are drawing in.

It's autumn now, and all around
The colours change, as they are bound
To herald yet another end
Of another year, which we did spend
Marvelling at nature's cycle,
Watching in wonder the yearly circle:

Winter, when all is resting calmly,
Except the weather, all but balmy;
Spring, when all comes back to life
With creatures pairing man and wife;
Summer, all aglow in sunshine
Days of roses and of wine;

But autumn is the best of all,
With nuts and conkers ripe to fall,
And berries glowing red and orange,
Fruit, and seeds across the range,
And colours standing out so clear,
Glorious sunsets, stars so near,
Morning mist and dewy grass,
All promise it will come to pass
That next year all begins anew,
And cycles back to autumn.

Joan E Milne

AUTUMN GOLD

Can it be this autumn time,
more beautiful than ever,
reminds me of a love from which
no season time could sever.

The leaves are dancing, twirling,
falling to the ground,
as the reassurance of your grace
that doesn't make a sound.

The trees are standing naked,
to endure the winter cold.
Hold me in your warm embrace
you never could withhold.

With flower petals falling
and chilly winds at night,
in the middle of storm clouds
I see a shining light.

The birds prepare for winter,
some fly to foreign lands.
I stay here by your side
you always understand.

Creation, multicoloured, patterns
the rainbow up above.
All agree and speak the truth
surely God is love.

Dorothy Brooks

Autumn's Fate

As our planet rotates
Away from the solar rays
Autumn's fate emerges
With her mellow jays.
The Earth's copper crust
Evokes her shrouded gown
Yield bare, silent trees
All hues of golden brown.
A cascade of tawny leaves
Decay, regress into the ground
Like laminated carpet sleeves
You hear the rustling sound.
Woody brambles entwined
Harvest blackberries so sweet
An oasis of fallen nuts
For creatures to store and eat.
Musky nights are longer
Her autumn days of dew
The shorter whispering grass
Barely a flower in view.
Children seek polished conkers
Animals prepare to hibernate
Busy bees become drowsy
In this autumn season's fate.

Patricia Carter

AUTUMN HARVEST

The senescent year gathers
its backdrops of chrysanthemum hues,
its orchards of burnished fruit
and its seas of golden wheat.

The chaff-fill'd air vibrates
to the hum of harvesters
sailing through the surf.

And, at voyage's end,
the festal celebration -
musical, ambrosian sustenance;

And the off'rings made to God
in thanksgiving.

Joy Morton

THE SEASON OF CHANGE

The heat has now gone out of the summer sun
And the touch of frost has just begun
When you wake up in the early morning
A shiver runs down your spine as the sheets stop warming

Now is the time to change the quilt
Put the heating on, sometimes up to the hilt.
A coal fire burning in the early night
Brings a warming feeling and a cosy sight

The curtains are now drawn soon after seven
And you are warm in bed not long after eleven
The days are shorter, but the nights are long
Christmas will be here before too long.

On reflection, nature too has her way to show
How autumn and its colours can bring a glow
Some leaves on trees change from green to gold
Other trees lose theirs, leaving outlines stark and bold

The squirrels hoard their nuts for the winter to come
Hedgehogs look for a warm hole to creep into for their home
Some birds prepare to leave their nests
I wish like them, I too could head west

Away to the sun-kissed countries far out of range
Do I really want to miss all the season's change?
No! I think we will stay just where we are,
Autumn has to be the most beautiful by far.

Sheila Storr

THE WILD FLOWER

Fair wild flowers of multi colour,
Your fragrance as sweet as a child's
Sweet demeanour.

You grow beneath the yellow leaves fall,
Oh carrier of life for insects to crawl.
The river flows so near to your edge,
To bring you life, for its soul's sacred pledge.

The sun filters through to give you your strength,
To dance in the wind, and multiply in length.
You spread your beauty for all to see,
So the woods give our race a place to be.

Thank you nature for showing us your story,
It's perfect in form and should take all the glory.
Without your presence life would be much less,
Without your care life would be in a mess.

Ricky N Lock

THIS SPLENDID AUTUMN DAY

We're drifting into autumn, a dry September day,
Some fluffy clouds outlined in blue, glide gently on their way.
Up above, I hear a plane, a helicopter too.
The plane makes lines of frosty white and disappears from view.
The noise of tractors droning, sounds distant on the breeze,
Joining the chirruping of birds and buzz of wasps and bees.
As I'm sitting browsing something catches my eye
I slowly turn my head and see rabbits feeding close by.
Soaking up the atmosphere time goes lazily by.
I'll not feel more contented no matter how I try.
What a lovely time of year. This splendid autumn day
Will be locked in my memory where it will always stay.

Margaret Doherty

A Beautiful Season

The once noisy 'dawn chorus' are reducing their volume,
We see signs of a sleepy hedgehog, seeking a new bedroom,
Lingering early morning mist, resembles a pointing finger,
And tussles with the rising sun as it fights to linger,
Silk lace, patterned shawls, adorned with pearls of dew,
Glisten on the hedges, giving a spectacular display to view.

Aerobatic swifts and swallows, for warmer climates leave,
Cool winds blow instead of a soft whispering summer breeze,
Yellows, reds, rusts and shades of brown mottled with green
As Mother Nature's new blanket, is everywhere to be seen
Children kick the crisp leaf carpets, shrieking with cries of delight
Sending a shower of colour, dancing and swirling, in hazy sunlight,

In our gardens, the rose's delicate scent, is now all spent too
Replaced by gold and bronze 'chrysanths' that show a different hue
Daylight quickly fades, a distinctive 'nip' in the air calls at dusk
That brings with it a strange odour, of damp pine-like musk
Every changing season, is the onset of another natural phase
But the wonder of autumn's beauty never ceases to amaze.

Glenice Siddall

AUTUMN

Red, yellow, green and gold
Now autumn's story is about to unfold
Wet leaves underfoot are an awful pest
On the trees they still look their best
Days are beginning to get quite short
Hunters begin to shoot for sport
Some birds start to fly away
While others come for their winter stay
After summer's heat the weather turns cool
Now some evenings you need a shawl
Winter will now soon be here
Bringing an end to another year.

June M Peek

AUTUMN

To hibernate,
Like many animals that do so year by year,
I'd really hate.
For I would miss the biting tang of frosty air,
And lacy cobwebs shimmering on branches bare,
And dark night sky alive with spangled stars so clear.

And I would miss
The joy of crunching through the fallen leaves,
The warm sun's kiss
Upon the earth to swell the ripened grain,
And knowing it is Harvest time again;
Rejoicing in the glorious golden sheaves.

And I'd miss too
The pungent smell of wood smoke from bonfires,
And every hue
Of colour, tints and shades of autumn all around,
As more leaves twist and twirl to meet the ground
To add more fuel to lingering burning pyres.

I would not know
When foggy days enshrouded all the earth,
Taking the glow
Of sunlit days and blanketing the country scene
In swirling mist and silence like a screen,
Foreshadowing winter's dearth.

Though I'd be warm,
And cosy sleeping in my burrow, lair or sett,
Safe from the storm,
I still would miss the mellow, autumn days
When summer has departed in a golden haze,
And winter has not shown his face as yet.

Brenda King

Autumn

Shades of gold on the leaves that fall
They leave the trees so bare to all.
The winds they blow in the autumn air
And gather up the leaves to fall in a heap.

A time of harvest for farmers all, to gather the golden corn.
Rosehips, blackberries ripe, laden full on the hedgerows.
Spiders' webs so fine and gleam like jewels in the morning sun.

Time to reflect on days gone by,
To walk with friends like the Canterbury Tales.
Leaves and bracken crack beneath our feet
Like fires and coal lying in a grate.

And when the day comes to a close
Darkness falls and then we sit beside our fires to keep us warm
And wait for the long days of spring's return.

W McLean

Autumn

Autumn winds
Coming in from the north
Bringing early frosts
November mists
Hiding any dangers ahead
Leaves coat the road
Like a gigantic ice rink
Mr Robin sits in his majestic pose
Watching and waiting
For those first ripening berries
From the great holly tree
With its luscious green leaves
That prickle like needles
For the unwary
The acorns are falling from the great oak
Crunching underfoot for the unsuspecting
While Mr Squirrel forages about
Roads litter'd with conkers
Chestnuts falling about
This autumn harvest
That nature supplies.

Patricia Turner

Autumn

The long hot summer has relinquished its grip,
lush green shades of leaves changing colours from their tips.
Autumn has arrived, nature's beauty manifest
hues of vivid red and yellow,
and pallid green mixtures in October's crest.

Cold nights reveal misty mornings heavy with dew
spiders' webs sparkling and resilient right through
silver shimmering droplets reflect the early morning sun
as if tears for nature flow and run.

Swirling mist in country lane
leaves fall gently, every autumn the same.
Summer birds have taken flight
the robin soon to face winter's plight.

Frost returns, as twilight falls,
a telling sign of winter's call;
leaves now crisp and brown
decaying on the ground.

Autumn fades into winter's term
and now all the leaves gone.
Woodland hedgerow thicket laid bare
waiting for spring to come next year.

David Stuart

SAND AND SUNFLOWERS
(Dedicated to my son, Christopher)

The summer's gone, it's autumn
But before I see it fade
What a summer it has been
Ice creams and buckets and spades.

And now the memories linger
Of the hottest day of the year
When the sun blazed down
On a seaside town
And we watched folk on the pier.

Long skirts, short skirts
Knotted hankies and hats
And folk with memories to tell
Who told us of days when they came there
And took their family as well.

But now I sit in my garden
The sun is still lovely and warm
The cats are sat under the garden chairs
It's too good to be indoors.

The berries are red on the bushes
Michaelmas daisy coming to life
A butterfly flutters overhead
I'm for this quiet life.

Not long ago it was Easter eggs
Now it's nearly November the fifth
When the bangers go off
And my peace is ruined
What happened to my bliss?

God grant me another winter
And strength to get through to the spring
And once again Earth rejoices
And the birds will once again sing.

Rachel Mary Mills

AUTUMN/WINTER

Brrr, said the breeze
as the autumn leaves
burnt themselves out
once again.

Fire and flame,
sun, shires and rain,
when the river grows cold
and the season starts to blow,
we have October, November, December and then:

Icicles, snowflakes, icebergs and frost,
old Jack with his colds and fires and his cough.

Spray, spit, fire and flight,
the wind and the sleet
sing through the night.

Winter slings some ice into a glass,
and I'm with an old friend
and we just while away the hours,
listening to the rattle of the storm and the showers.

M C Jones

THE PORTRAIT

She waits in the 'wings' brush poised like Monet's
Paint palette overflows with flames - golds and reds
As soon with a flourish while awaiting her cue
To be called with her canvas - autumn season is due
Impatient yet eager she's waited so long
As summer kept autumn on hold with her song
The mists met the trees still shimmering green
Reluctant warm sunshine - autumn lady deceives
But with gentle persuasion she starts on her quest
Quietly at first brushes - tip the first hedge
To enhance changing colours - this is her pledge.

Like the circle of life increasing the pace
With reckless abandon the desire is to race
Provide vivid colours - magical powers unfold
Unseen we all wonder this joy to behold
Eager and forceful exhausted yet proud
Her picture complete - takes a bow from the clouds
We watch and we wait, her skills unfulfilled
The carpet is yet to be laid as leaves yield
Crisp 'neath our feet - colours still bright
Autumn lady delivers another delight.

Do we all ever wonder this dream to inspire
As small eager fingers trace colours of fire.
This artistic reflection lay dormant and new
With a smile she retreats her work is on view
The lady's portrait of colour was long overdue.

Irene Siviour

AUTUMN

Autumn leaves start to fall
From trees, small and high above our heads
Fluttering, weaving, turning
Before our very eyes,
Falls to the ground
You don't hear a sound,
Till the change of climate
From warm to cold, leaves turn deeper in colour
Amber, golden yellow, browns, red
Turns our heads,
To see the splendour, of God's creation
The autumn leaves,
On trees, houses, historic buildings,
We pick them up, touch the leaves
See their veins, that can weep
When squeezed, and pressed at our fingertips
Or a blow from the lips, are like fairies
Dancing in the breeze,
Winter gets colder, leaves get crisper
Disintegrates into ash, when burnt to a smoulder,
For compost, to make great fertilisation
The leaves that fall beneath our feet
Artists, photographic societies, school children
Study the beautiful autumn leaves.

Norma Flair Challis

MISTY SATURDAY MORNING

As I look across the rooftops
Beyond the fading trees
At the leafless leafy suburb
In a stillness with no breeze.

No traffic or no people
The shutters are still down
And the precinct so deserted
In this misty market town.

This misty Saturday morning
With its blend of larch and yew
In the peacefulness of autumn
Across the field of dew.

Neville Anthony

AUTUMN

The air is crisp, the morning fresh,
The time of the day that I like the best,
A walk in the woods to the crackle of leaves,
And to see the reds and gold of those on the trees,
There are berries for the birds and humans too,
Nature's promise of fulfilment has come true,
The orchards are full of apples, pears and plums,
Just waiting for the pickers to come,
The flowers are slowly fading away,
And bees and butterflies shorten their stay,
The days get shorter as onward we go,
To colder weather and maybe some snow,
Fires burn brightly and curtains are drawn,
No one will move now until the morn,
The gardens are bare now the work's all done,
So nature and man now will rest,
Until the spring comes.

M G Clements

AUTUMN

He creeps in stealthily
A chill, a scarf
A change of birdsong
Cheeks gain glows healthily
A falling leaf
A shadow long

The sun still warm
Slowly says goodbye
And darkness sits upon the sky
We fondly kiss the sun adieu
As golden tones address the eye

The indolent heat
Evaporates with a sigh
Rich in gold, approaching fast
Autumnal tones
The summer past.

Lesley McDonagh

SEPTEMBER SISTERS

I know it's autumn when the girls are back
In patterned coats and stockings striped with black.
All at once I see them hanging out
Watchfully assessing who's about
From chosen vantage point in sun or shade
Motionless: no overt rush for trade.

These sisters have their indoor counterpart
Long-limbed and swift with looks to stop the heart.
No bashful wallflowers these - they eat their men
When they have had their evil way with them.
Or so I'm told not having researched wider
This is all I know about the spider.

Linda D'Alessio

NOVEMBER DAY

This loon-spun morning like a strayed cat
Talks illusion
Through dead lettered streets
And steals a march across the scuttled mat
Of colours run
At the numbed sap's release.

Through moted eye she censors day's chill
Repertory.
Hers to suppress
All movement, slur the barely uttered will
On a furled sky
In shramm'd still wilderness.

With fastidious gloved-clay pad the thief?
Smothers high noon
Whose powered shadows stand
Time cancelled in a blind motif;
No lector's pun
Their slanting hours to ground.

All is half tone, colourless as sorrow
For unknown sake.
Pilot sightlessly mocks
Celebrant at barrow
Limp, stifled wake
Holding while crib unlocks.

From the basin's slopped out cavity
No welling stream
Compasses light,
No gleam kindles the grotto'd eye
Haunting damp requiem
Drip-dripped into night.

Norah Green

AUTUMN LEAVES

Leaves stirred by a stiffening breeze,
Dislodge from weary parent trees.
One by one, they flutter down
Red and yellow, orange and brown
Dragged home by hedgehog, mouse and vole
To keep nests warm during winter's snow
Shuffling feet make a crunchy sound
Through the dense carpet on the ground.
All around us leaves are lying,
Showing that the year is dying.
Soon all the branches will be bare
There'll be no green foliage anywhere
Autumn is a time of deceleration
Let's anticipate springtime's rejuvenation.

G D Furse

AUTUMN OF LIFE

We all change as we grow older
I am the first to admit this
Most of us do this with reasonable grace
But a few cannot accept being dismissed
Why is it some of our heroes
Decidedly let themselves go
When their days of sporting prowess
End in retirement woe
Now comparisons are said to be odious
So I shall never reveal the names
Of some sadly neglected figures
Once they say farewell to fame
Then, obese from overeating
Faces flushed from too much wine
The lines of dissatisfaction
Etch furrows on foreheads with time
Please have enough pride in your past life
To preserve the image right through to full time.

Barbara Williams

AUTUMN LEAVES

Leaves they scatter all around,
The crunching sound,
Brown, decaying veins, hard and cold,
Autumn is quite bold.

The children kick the fallen leaves,
The crunching sound.

Now, the rain came,
Sogging sap.
Trees, they are all bare.
Sticks strike the bark.

The wind brings them tumbling down.
Tumbling, tumbling,
Crashing to the ground,
The crunching sound

Stark trees now stand,
Autumn, she really is quite bold.

Maria Ann Cahill

ONE AUTUMN DAY

As I passed through the wood,
a gentle cloud floated down
and lay twisted and curled at my feet.

The silent cloud became audible,
as it crackled and crunched beneath me.

The twisted, curled shapes,
once so fresh, green and translucent
lay dead, on the woodland floor.

The living, green canopy,
that gave shade from the sun,
its time now spent,
shrouded the earth.

Yet, I was surrounded by beauty,
of colour, shape and sound,
as the leaves found their final resting place.

Joan Thompson

A Season

Breath of God
Soothing the troubled gusts
That spring from sources
Deep as time.
Melting miseries
Of dying snowflakes
Resembles autumn leaves,
As they too return to the earth
Their time ended,
Their beauty dead.
Face of winter
Form of feeling
That once again
The dark and bitterness return,
With eyes of night
They skim and hunt,
Staring at the rose of morning,
Whose petals have lost their quiet grace
And now lay wild and tossed,
Torn by their own thorns
As they fell.

Julie Spackman

AUTUMN

A wonderful time of year.
Sun in the sky,
But a breeze flies by.
Crunch, crunch of the leaves on the ground,
That have fallen from trees all around.
The warning that winter is on its way,
That is an autumn's day.

Nicole Woollard

Autumn Term

Natural imagery proved too much for the man
True he was comfortable with images of the natural world
                                                            in literature
It was, after all, his job.
But walking to work
At the start of yet one more term
An old leaf falling induced a feeling of slow
                                           and ineffable sadness . . .

Dai Blatchford

AUTUMN

Our long hot summer slowly fades.
The nights draw in, the sky canvas alters.
A slight chill in the air.
The trees start to change and sway.
Crumpled leaves on the path underfoot
Like a blanket cascading down.
Crane flies appear.
Morning dew on the flowers.
The sun appears through the clouds.
Children go back to school,
Crawling out of bed, no more saying, I'm bored.
The transitional part of the year
Our old friend autumn.

Michelle Elliott

SEASON OF SILENCES

One long, lovely summer
once I spent with you
till fallen angels broke cover;
enter autumn, on cue

Our time together near over,
we were as leaves
on a grieving sycamore
falling like tears

Drifting, piling on a grave
of broken promises,
all the love we'll never have
for all our kisses

Saddest of autumn dreams,
unspoken poems.

R N Taber

AUTUMN

Autumn is here again
A season later in the year
A time to gather in harvest grain
It is a time of much gladness and cheer

Because change in scenery is going on
Breathtaking changes in colour of leaves abound
Birds singing on the tree branches they sit upon
Happy harvesters reaping as they sing aloud

Everyone happy with the turn out of crops
Reaping food crops for good health
Fill up the shelves in the shops
Loving every hardworking hour to produce food for health and wealth

Time to bring in produce of the land has begun
Environment where autumn leaves change from green to orange
                                                                                                  to brown
A cooler climate now that summer has gone
Planning to sell produce in the country and in town.

Olive May McIntosh-Stedman

NOVEMBER

Is a pond in the afternoon
    the tops of birches
incandescent, their massed saffron
smashed in the water as by brush
    or thumb, to a blink.
It is dogwood, a scarlet mesh
trimmed apple-green, bending beside
    the pond's darkest creek.
It is the water lily tied
in its flotilla, half-asleep;
    an oak letting fall
bronze leaves into the tearful cup
to meet their reflections, to sail.

I go there often at this time
    to gather myself
near painted water's knurl and rhyme
and be refreshed as by a drink,
    as by a smooth sleep.
Beside the dogwood I can think
at the pace of clouds, silver through
    my own commotion -
and soon afterwards, as I go
through night-time streets with the heckle
    and brag of traffic,
I build spirit with my recall
of those treetops, that waterwork.

Chris White

AUTUMNIC SORROW

Delicate sound whispers an autumnal call
forestalling the swallows in their enchantment,
sent in a song to stimulate leaf fall
recalling a concord by way of enticement,
persuading a sorrow to come to the fore
follow the swifts to a migratory shore,
open a note for the north winds embarkment
within seasonal descent upon forest floor.

Drew Hawfawn

Rise

As the early sun rises and stains the sky blue and grey,
I lay in my bed, dreaming smells of porridge, toast and coffee.
Sunbeams skate over cloudy skies,
Their pure, full lips kiss my eyes with arterial orange,
So I turn away and hide my face under the sheets.
Icicles drip, waters slowly drain
And leaves run the race down from the trees.
It's the month that autumn begins falling asleep.

Gary Raymond

Autumn

September, October, November,
Crimson, purple and gold,
Bright colours these to remind us
The year is growing old.

The robin comes back to the garden,
The smell of burning leaves
Tells gardeners are stoking their bonfires
While farmers gather their sheaves.

Apples, nuts and brambles
Where blossom used to cling,
Autumn brings fulfilment
To the promises of spring.

Coralie Campbell

GLORIOUS AUTUMN

Glorious autumn,
Always the same,
When again autumn comes to the lane.
Hedgerows' leaves, lovely rusty russet gold.
Summer exhausted, and now looking old.
Plentiful blue-black fruits on the sloe.
Gardener's spades take over from the hoes.
Abundance red berries on the hawthorns.
Dripping with moisture on chilly, misty morn.
Woolly jumpers over cotton nylon.
Housemartins from the skies, long gone.
Look forward to their return in spring.
Content with a harvest festival hymn,
From the chapel, one hears, gathering sing.
That lifts one's heart.
From this summer, sadly depart.
Year by year, ongoing thing,
Autumn again, then awaiting for spring.

George B Clarke

AUTUMN

Why am I cast down and despondently sad
When I long to be happy and joyous and glad?
Why is my heart heavy with unfathomable weight
As I try to escape this soul saddened state?
I ask myself often - what makes life this way,
Why is the song silenced in the heart that was gay?
And then with God's help it all becomes clear,
The soul has its seasons, just the same as the year.

I too must pass through life's autumn of dying,
A desolate period of heart-hurt and crying,
Followed by winter in whose frost-bitten hand
My heart is as frozen as the snow-covered land -
Yes, man too must pass through the seasons God sends,
Content in the knowledge that everything ends,
And oh what a blessing to know there are reasons
And to find that our soul must too have its seasons -
Bounteous seasons and barren ones too,
Times for rejoicing and times to be blue,
But meeting these seasons of dark desolation
With strength that is born of anticipation
That comes from knowing that 'autumn time sadness'
Will surely be followed by a 'springtime of gladness'.

R Vincent

THE MIST OF THIS AUTUMN MORNING

The shimmering mist pervades this autumn morning.
The earth breathes out the dreams of generations long dead
For it took in their bodies at the soul's crossing
And consumed the residue that was left.
Something was retained from the cold brain,
Which drained into the surrounding soil
Into the cracks and crevasses,
As searching as a snake of oil.
A residual memory remained.
Whose ancient thoughts might be ascertained
By those attuned to the gentle breeze of June
Or in the chill of late October's gloom
When dark storms raged beneath forbidden skies
And when the stars' bright eyes spy down
On the wayward ways of a midnight town.
Old memories stir, long buried events recur.
Ancient doors open, and the unwary
Take fright at the sight of ghosts
Or the more enlightened are entertained by angels.
Such benign, kindly, heavenly hosts.
They are but time reacted scenes
As the slumbering land remembers
Events, times spent, whilst she wistfully dreams.
The good times, the bad times, what once had been.
From long gone centuries and recent decades,
Repeatedly replayed,
Until worn and decayed they fade away.
As ephemeral as autumn mist, they quietly drift,
Then by the dawn's light, by sunlight dismissed.

Jonathan Pegg

AUTUMN MASSACRE

What is it about autumn?
That makes it my favourite season.
Why do I look forward so much?
Surely there must be a reason?

Is it the mildness of the evenings?
Listening to all the birds sing?
Or sitting at home in front of the fire
As the nights start drawing in.

The colours of the dying leaves perhaps?
All brown, yellow and red.
Or is it that the summer wasps
Will soon all be dead?

Eifion Thomas

Autumn Is Here

Crunch, crunch goes the leaves,
as the postman walks up the path
vibrant colours, all new smells
as the starling has a bath.
Where are the lambs? They have gone,
summer's nearly gone too
so has baby birds and baby bees
they have gone away and flew
something's coming, can you see it?
Bringing animals like deer
all new colours, all new smells
autumn is here.

Stacey Weeks-Pearson

October

When autumn with her ageing hand
Casts a long spell upon the land,
She sets no scene of sombre grey
But weaves the woods with colours gay.

For though the weeks are waxing old
There comes again an age of gold;
Earth years for festival a gown
Of yellow, russet, red and brown.

The fruitful tree, the nut-clad hedge
To time of plenty give their pledge,
Apple and hop and grape-great vine
Liquors distil of taste divine.

Then you who three score autumns know
Greet these ripe years with gladdened glow,
Let sagess crown your snowy hair
And boldly all life's fullness share.

Teach all the world forgotten truth -
Not every prize belongs to youth;
For steadfast souls still waits a boon
By silvery light of harvest moon.

Barrie Williams

AUTUMN, IN AN ENGLISH WOOD

Autumn, in an English wood.
How quick the change, from when we stood
'Neath canopies green, spreading overhead
But now the shades are brown and red.

So cool the air, so cold the breeze
Gusting wings quaver falling leaves.
Rehearsing the troupe of red and brown
As tumble and dance, they pirouette down.

Shadows longer, days are short,
A rainbow leaps, but soon is caught
By chasing clouds, that shield the sun from view
Causing raindrops to spatter, on the oak and yew.

Where once we walked and once, we kissed,
The path we shared now veiled, in mist.
Cloudy skies hide our shooting star,
Our wish has gone, but where, how far?

Now grey and drab my walking hours.
No scenic views of scented flowers.
No mating pairs, with joys to sing,
It's autumn's touch, on everything.

Seasonal hues of chestnut gold,
When, will summer's shades unfold.
Open her palette, colour each bud,
But now it's autumn, in an English wood.

Gordon Wilson

AUTUMN GLADNESS

Now the trees stand in autumn gladness
A soft breeze blows away all my sadness
Above me lonely seagulls fly
Lost against a cloudy sky
The last lovely blossom
Falls reluctantly to the floor
Where lies a leafy carpet
Spreading before winter's door
As the sun pierces through
The silent sounds of sweet decay
Another year sleeps gently away.

Linda Doel

AN AUTUMN DAY

As I peer through the window
On a sultry autumn afternoon
My thoughts gather momentum
Of a summer gone too soon.

The trees are all leafless
Stripped back to the bare
Blowing leaves and raindrops
Being tossed in the gathering air.

Everything looks so dowdy
Grass is overgrown
Shopping bags and rubbish
Into corners often blown.

Gates that open and close
Without anybody there
Take a walk in the rainfall
But only for a dare.

We are all feeling miserable
As winter has yet to come
Longing for the blue skies
And the days of a summer sun.

Geoffrey Graham

ANOTHER ODE TO AUTUMN

The actress year applies her paint
To stage her autumn show.
Polychromatic, nothing faint,
She shows her face aglow.

An unkind critic sees decay
As she takes centre-stage
But brave old year presents her play
And lies about her age.

Familiar though the play may be
It still has much to teach,
And all who come to hear and see
Join in the closing speech.
'Our life is soil beneath the plough.
The furrows that we walk between
Are longed-for things that might have been
Or things that never can be now.
There is no harvest to be won
From youth's unsown wild oats
And neither light nor heat is gained
From fleets of unburned boats.'

J Morley

AUTUMN
(After Belle Ëpoque)

Autumn brushes
Cider coloured leaves from her hair
Chases dancing leaves
Barefooted over grass
Damp with dew
As winter prepares
For winter chills
And swirling snow
Sheltering
In summer's memories

Paul Wilkins

AUTUMN TIME

Autumn is a lovely time,
of new beginnings,
and the shedding of the old.
It's especially welcomed;
as the summer has been,
very hot and stifling.
It will be time to gather
back with family indoors.
Time to cooking meals once again.
Of course it will be sad
not to sit in the outdoors,
watching the birds, greenery and flowers.
Such an idyllic season is summer,
with the splendid shining sun,
and sweet song of the birds.
But little is meant to be forever
and autumn is a lovely, golden season.
Time to start anew,
to ponder and reflect,
on all that's good and lovely.
Time for a change of clothing
and for long walks amidst the golden leaves.
Reminding us that summer has faded
and onward we must go.
But we needn't lose heart,
because, God willing,
we shall be here again next year.
Where autumn time will start again
and who knows what possibilities will unfold.

Christina Gilbert

Autumn Is Here

Things feel different as I walk in the countryside, I see so many things that have changed.
The leaves are turning to that beautiful colour of brown and gold.
I smile as they fall from the trees as if they have a will of their own.

I stand and watch the leaves falling onto the path, wishing to capture every moment in my memory.
With every fall of every leaf it reminds me that autumn has arrived.

In place of the sun is the frost, it glistens on the path that I now walk.
It rests on leaves making them shimmer, looks like Jack Frost is about again.

The rain keeps falling and I am soaking wet.
Why am I so happy in this dreadful state?
Could it be the dog that walks by my side, with happiness etched in his face or is it a time to be happy with the world?

With the changing of weather, as the months pass by, it brings with it excitement.
What will the autumn bring this year?
Love, sadness, heartache!
Only time will tell as the days pass by at a rapid rate.

Lisa Platts

CIDER DAYS

They came from all around with apples,
gauzy shirts and jeans and crystals in their hair,
bringing jars with bits of grot and spiders.
A golden day with the thrum of wasps
and bumblebees and summer's
leftover dragonflies.
Beneath the apple trees that were laden
with russet and green and gold,
Children with half eaten apples,
crouched and jumped and hid
in the long sweet smelling grass.
Men in Cargoes and Velcro-strapped sandals,
heaved the press around and around,
whilst the juice ran.
Golden and plentiful for the children to drink
with sweet lips and laughing eyes,
beneath the sugar-sweet spout as it flowed,
in a fountain of sunshine that drowned their hair.
They filled all the bottles, two hundred
or more and five hundred wasps.
As the crowd baked bread and
the brick oven smoked
and they laughed with cameras clicking,
To the sound of autumn's children.

Robyn Dalby-Stockwell

THE FRUIT OF AUTUMN

Plundered just before the killer frost
Our garden lies resting in a ruinous heap
The final fruit of autumn having flown away
To safely perch upon a cosy kitchen sill
To turn from tart to sweet.

Fingerstreaks of sparkling frost
In sinister pursuit
Adorn the outer window glass
And seem to reach in vain
To claim the season's final fruit.

James Rasmusson

AN AUTUMN QUINTILE

Mare's tails
Drifting behind
Halo'ed clouds, flecked on
Equinox autumnal evening
Sunset
to
Bonfired
November month
Of temperatures low
Layered rolls of dank liquid fog
Widespread
over
This earth
This mortal coil
Seeming complete, fulfilled
Yet each year, newborn life nature
Renews

Brian Strand

AUTUMN

Sad how summer
slips her moorings
and drifts away; driven
by autumn whose artist's
hands, having turned
trees to torches
will suddenly
strip them of leaves
turning branches to whips
that lash the November
skies;
autumn's no friend:
the colours he paints
are nothing more
than a clown's mask
concealing
the white face
of winter.

Alan Millard

September Days

I much prefer September days,
Which often start with mist or haze.

Almost autumn, but not quite,
The cooler days can still delight.

Despite the sun there's a nip in the air,
Some days are like summer, mild and fair.

Other days may be tranquil and calm,
Awaiting the coming of winter's harm.

Older folk take their holidays then,
When the school term begins again.

As there are late flowers in bloom,
Bees are busy, in and out they zoom.

The evenings are fast drawing in,
Spiders, their webs, begin to spin.

Trees change the colours of their leaves,
Golden corn is stacked in tidy sheaves.

Churches everywhere celebrate Harvest,
Where local produce comes to be blest.

Birds that visit in summer will migrate,
While small animals start to hibernate.

The time to take up a new hobby or craft,
And enjoy dark evenings with a new heart.

A much needed space to relax and unwind,
Before thoughts of Christmas spring to mind!

Rosemary Davies

Autumn

In all its burnished glory
Leaves falling to the ground
At first floating silently
Drifting without a sound.

Rich colours, copper and yellows
On the ground unfurl
Lay there, deep and crisp
Winds make them dance and swirl.

Quietly summer slips away
Replaced by days, rich and golden
This is the gift of nature
For which we are beholden.

Arms outstretched
Stripped of all their glory
The trees wait silently
To begin again their story.

Suzanne Thorne

Autumn

Autumn wears her rich velvet cloak,
And twirls to show off her colours
Of red, orange, amber and brown,
As she passes through the trees.
Then she heads across the fields,
Golden corn droops its weary head,
And the ground becomes dull and bare
As the last crop is harvested.

Autumn sprinkles her bright jewels
Of deep red and purple berries
In the fading leafy headgerows,
Beneficent in her passing.
The sleepy warmth of the still air
Changes at her journey's finish,
Turning to the chill and greyness
Of winter who is following fast.

Gilly Jones-Croft

Autumn

Summer flowers are slowly fading,
Early morning mists are here,
Seasons are forever changing,
Summer goes and autumn's near.

Soon the vibrant colours show,
Of the varied leaves,
Orange, bronze, reds and gold,
As nature decks the trees.

Wheat is safely gathered in,
Wood smoke scents the air.
Harvest moon is on the rise,
Peace for all to share.

E Timmins

NATURE'S ESSENCE

Summer packs her bags
And walks away
Remnants of sun-kissed days
Wave the hand
Air pierced with a stranger
Crisp coolness

Transforming trees
Bronzed beauties
Showing and glowing
In the deep red sky

Crunchy carpet lay
Beneath every foot
Lively leaves
Proudly portray
An autumn day

Brown hazels fall
A squirrel's delight
Quick bury them deep
With your little feet!

Temperature rises
Artificial heat
Warms pleasurably
Cold hands and feet.

The coming of Jack
Fast approaching
As nature prepares
For a beating
The cold, frosty phantom

Now looming . . .

Kerry Webber

AUTUMN IS COMING

Autumn is coming, there's a chill in the morning air.
Leaves on trees are changing colour, soon they'll start to fall,
Children have returned to school to start a new school year!
Lots of things to talk about after a long summer break.
Soon they will be walking through deep piles of crisp leaves,
Throwing sticks to dislodge conkers,
Bonfires will soon be built and fireworks ignited,
Rockets shooting into the night sky
Days are getting shorter, soon dark nights will be here.
Thoughts will turn to Christmas and what will Santa bring!

Rita E Sturdy

THE AUTUMN SCENE

The leaves are in a medley of gold,
yellow, brown and red.
The fields worn thin by the cattle
who have assuredly tread.
Farmers ploughing
have left a bare brown and white
flint, showing through.
Excitable squirrels skip in front of you,
High above the trees
cluster of birds get ready for the
winter freeze.
Robins sit firmly in the hedges
watching quizzically!
Half unconsciously, the sheep
are munching from end to end
of the fields.
And more quickly, the sun begins to yield
on the dormain.
The season of autumn slowly creeps up on us, once again.

Sammy Michael Davis

AUTUMN

The summer is disappearing,
The trees' leaves are falling.
Crunching under my feet,
As I stroll along the street.

The sun is setting faster at night,
The darkness is here again,
And so is the pouring rain.

It's colder in the morning,
As I walk out with the dog.
Warming my hands with my breath
And fighting through the fog.

Spider webs on the fields of grass
Shimmering the morning dew.
Autumn is here at last
Can't wait to share Christmas with you!

Jackie Sutton

MOTHER NATURE'S TREASURE CHEST

Summer has gone
It is finally over
No more green fields of luscious clover
Daisies and buttercups - all are gone
Until next year
Now autumn is here
With its golden glow
And the leaves falling from the trees.
One by one they flutter down
To the damp and cold ground below
A carpet that rustles and crackles
Beneath our feet as we trudge along
Over our carpet of gold.
The birds now fly to warmer climes
And the bees - no buzzing inside their hives.
Less humming and droning from now on,
No honey left, the flowers are gone.
Goodbye summer
We'll miss you so
At least there's always autumn's glow,
Until cold winter comes along
Then the air is filled with Christmas
Melodies and song
And summer is a long way off, once more -
The season that we all adore.

Margaret McHugh

Autumn On Cannock Chase

Our tiny cottage on the hills,
Where linnets sang in tinkling trills,
Where rabbits raced and harebells blew
And bilberry bushes also grew;
The hills festooned with blackberries rich,
We stood on tiptoe in the ditch,
The ripest ones were higher still,
We teased them down and had our fill!
Silky grasses, gorse and heather,
Purple tufts, ferns brown as leather,
Autumn was the busiest time,
Gathered sticks, beneath the lime:
Picked ripe damsons, plums and quince,
Stirred the chutney to go with mince!
Apples, pears, were ripe and red,
Nature's bounty, home-made bread:
We wheeled our cart to pick up wood,
Our toffee apples tasted good!
Before the wind began to race,
We hurried home at running pace;
Mother peeled and cooked her wares,
Soon the shelves groaned unawares
Of other treasures, chestnuts round,
Hazelnuts and beechnuts found
Then horse chestnut, last of all,
Lined them up against the wall,
Left to dry, we hoped to beat
Our playmates in the village street;
Tiny cottage, standing still,
Near the wood, beside the rill,
Purple heather, sage and thyme,
Remembered joys, a happy time!

Norma Rudge

Our Day

Golden mists of autumn;
Dark fruits upon the trees;
The last few swallows
Circle 'round,
In flight, so gracefully.

Dew upon
Each leaf and flower
Reflecting
Pale blue skies,
Colours so rich and varied
Bring joy to mind
And eyes.
Deep reds
Like embers burning,
Greens of ev'ry hue,
Burnished golds
Gild and shine
As treasure that is stored.

Within God's wondrous
Framework
And nature's healing power,
To watch
And see these glories -
Pure pleasure
Hour by hour.

Lyn Sandford

A Season To Treasure

Autumn is the time of year,
That I love most of all.
When vibrant leaves of red and gold
Slowly start to fall.
With squirrels foraging for food,
To add to their winter's store,
A blustery wind stings my face,
And chills me to the core.
It's a time to think of cosy nights,
Warm in the fire's glow,
A time to sort the garden out,
Before the winter's snow.
I hear a lonely blackbird's cry,
From my garden wall,
Yes, autumn is the time of year
That I love most of all.

Carol Bond

Autumn

I know not whence it came
this sudden dash of bronze
just as the sun,
with the lightest touch,
kissed the outer leaves
of a nearby tree;
blackberries glistening
in the afternoon sun.
And suddenly I knew
that autumn was near,
felt the chill in the air
of early morning mist,
the need for a source
of light and warmth;
for the homeliness
of the hearth.

Time to reflect

now in my time of life
Autumn has come.

Josepha Blay

ANTICIPATING AUTUMN

Notice first a gentle falling of the leaves
And perspiration on the windows, early dawn
The appearance of grey squirrels in the trees
Old Chestnuts' bloated fruits, ready now to spawn

Yet clinging still to warmth of summer's past
Suburban flora in magnificence remains
The knowledge that this beauty cannot last
Stays hidden 'til a change in that fickle weathervane

Aware now of subtle differences at daybreak
Gone, the many voices of our feathered kin
Petals fast upon the ground present in opaque
Preparing sustenance for all that lies within

Recognise the chillness hanging round at eventide
See the dewy cobwebs that were previous hid away
Led on by Mother Nature's personal hand-picked guide
To watch the special birthing of this new autumnal day

Anticipate the richness of the season just ahead
Enjoy new revelations that only autumn brings
Prepare to meet its many challenges, instead
Of allowing autumn blues to spread its wings

Sandra Griesbach

AUTUMN ACROSS THE BARRICADES

Dream on dream along the path
To see rows of rusty leaves
Lying on the ground musty, misty
Ghost writer, fierce fighter for Keat's Autumn

Trees, tall, touch the sky
Misty morning smell over the river
Appeals to the sense of wellness in Britain
Necessary experience succulent taste

Air damp, feel the finger of autumn
Commentator sits ready for the off
Golden brown, rust red, shine out
Autumn leaves on the walk to the water

Give us a loaf of bread or force fed on poetry
Trees laden, apple store like squirrels hoard wealth
Careless of innocents abroad
Begin again at the Cathedral garden

Let's go to the wishing well across the barricades
Look down into the deep pool of water
Mirror image of yourself with Roisin
Sun hangs low over El Camino Real

All the way to San José
Most beautiful scene in America
Autumn, wear that woolly sweater
Sky clear blue all those days spent in motion

Blind to the touch of your hand
Believer in the natural order
Move on up to the top executive class
Autumn across the barricades

Shine on harvest moon
On the earth below my feet.

S M Thompson

Our Autumn Years

Autumn is the evening, as the day that's almost gone,
Autumn is the evening of the year.
A comforting season when now it's time to rest,
Like the day, the summer's gone and peace is here.

Autumn, as in life, a retiring time for most,
Resigning from the hard work of the rage.
It is bliss to think to pause and play the host,
Of the interlude that these autumn years have paged.

Autumn, colours subtle, as the leaves we change our locks,
Not staying as the power of summer's strength.
The beauty of the shades are seen in gentle folk,
As the sun shines through the leaves in evening's length.

Evenings are the rest time, an important part of life,
We can all enjoy the beauty that autumn's brought.
We carpet the world before the wintertime,
Now relax after the summer works are fought.

This gentle autumn fall and the weakening morning sun,
Just waiting for the love that we can give.
And then when night comes and the tranquil day is done,
You will know that this autumn is yours to live.

Lucy Bloxham

Autumn Concerto

When summer disappears
Then autumn takes the stage
And in the book of seasons
Will turn another page

A pleasant overture
Comes softly into play
Where there maybe late flowers
And birds who wish to stay

Next we hear the woodwind
A light, soft, swishing sound
As floating leaves and petals
Fall, carpeting the ground

The last ripe fruit is gleaned
As street lamps blur with mist
Autumn's concerto begins
And cooler days persist

A gentle breeze at first
That sounds just like a sigh
'Til stormy grey clouds gather
Within a leaden sky

Torrential downpours spread
A sigh becomes a roar
The wind, a loud crescendo
Across the Earth's soaked floor

Decrescendo at last
As blessed silence falls
A temporary prelude
'Til the next season calls!

Patricia Whittle

Los Colores Del Otoño
(The Colours Of Autumn)

Beneath the canopy of the heavens, all things must change,
And with the fall of autumn comes nature's time to rearrange.
The mighty sun, a little weary from his daily summer dance
across the sky,
Rises a little later and climbs not quite so high.
The warming rays which nourish earth, grow ever weaker by the day,
And autumn reaches out to the earth its own symphony to play.

The ocean waves in the crystal bay are no longer quite so blue,
As the sun yawns in its weariness, they assume a darker hue.
The seabirds wheel and whirl and then are gone in vast formation,
Like pilgrims they must chase the sun in their annual migration.
And from those who stay here all year round there is heard a song
of expectation,
As autumn heralds the coming of winter's grip of stark privation.

A cascade of wrinkled, dying leaves falls from the branches of trees
too tired to care,
As their branches reach skywards imploringly for a warmth
no longer there.
So green turns to shades of red, to russet and to brown,
As nature releases the season's growth and lays its rustling carpet down.
The creatures of the forest prepare quarters for their winter salvation,
Some turn away from the greying world and descend into hibernation.

The clouds which danced across the sky are no longer quite so white,
They twist in the ever growing wind and run away as if in fright.
They are blown into oblivion but just as quickly are replaced,
By their dark, grey, rain-filled cousins, by whom they are displaced.
In the season of the dying sun the earth itself appears to shiver,
White frost fingers reach out and place a dusting of ice on the
mountain river.

The mighty sun climbs ever slower in the greying sky each day,
As the vibrant colours of autumn mock his efforts in every way.
For even the sun with all its might must bow before the fall,
And autumn, with grim rectitude, casts its growing shadows
like a shawl,
The blues and greens of summer are soon no more than a distant dream,
King Winter will soon be here again, but for now, we are touched
by his queen!

Juan Pablo Jalisco

Autumn

Leaves are falling from the trees
Wasps are going, so are the bees
Sun is shining, low in the sky
Rubbish is swirling way up high
Hedgerows, red and bronze and gold
It's beginning to feel a little cold
The sunset is a lovely sight
Red and gold in the evening light
Autumn is my favourite season
Happy memories that is the reason
Chill in the mornings, then turning warm
Typical and true to form
This is the only time that you will see
                                                  such shades
In autumn - when summer fades
Brown, red, all kinds of green
Truly magnificent that has to be seen
Autumn is a pleasant time of year
Summer now over, winter is near.

Ethel Wakeford

PARKLAND KING

Resplendent king,
Mighty oak,
Your stance is true and proud.
Below your subjects
In autumn's grasp,
Pay homage to your might.
Cherry gnarled, Acer fine,
Maple's hues ignite.
All adorn your age-claimed ground,
With windswept jewels of gold and bronze.
Rubies and amethysts,
Amber's delight,
Like gossamer feathers,
All do take flight.
Mighty oak,
Resplendent and proud,
How mottled with autumn
Is your canopy shroud.
From your wind-torn ramparts,
From your mantle tall,
Look down at your subjects,
And your jewel-laden shawl.

Martyn Reed

SPRING

When do the leaves appear on the trees,
one day they are so bare
the next you look and stare.
They have appeared by magic overnight,
leaves so green,
fresh and new,
blossom covers the ground,
so perfect and silent without a sound,
winter is over, spring is here.
The light nights and warm days of summer are near,
dark nights and grey days are in the past.
Cold days of winter have gone at last,
the new seasonal shift,
gives our souls a lift,
makes us happier inside,
as the dark days of winter subside.

Jennifer Park

AUTUMN

I miss my autumn bonfire,
Symbol of death and rebirth.
Blazing heat against my face,
The smell of wood and earth.
Burn. Burn it all,
Dead leaves and weeds
Crumbling will fall
Into piles of silver ash.
Burn all night - burn all!

Diana Stannus

HARVEST TIME

To let us get at the point
we often seem to miss, that familiarity
brings *contentment,* there has to be
a harvest time.
Earth is not concerned with experiment,
nor scorning of constancy with maturity,
but lets each year's crop grow
the same as the last and bends the knee
to the habitual, to a beauty that is never marred,
sees in each dear old flower a new worth
and joys in meeting a familiar friend.
We remember the May blossom
snubbing a nose at the past winter
in a mockery of white
while the new shoots of spring,
their heads down, wait to charge.
We love the meadows, green again
as those our ancestors ran in,
and the open-handed flowers that display
a declaration of petals
so the puff clouds of summer can scatter
next year's seeds across the fields.
Though for the moment the hedgerows here
seem lost in a high-grown tangle
of couch grass, briar, dock and thistle,
we know that autumn's Parthian shot
will fire off a last acclamation of decadent beauty,
that winter will bring a cleansing,
then a beginning, in which familiar frame
our joy will be undiminished.

Richard Unwin

Autumn's Tapestry

Autumn's the countdown season of the year,
When summer guests at nature's grand hotel
Pack, pay and then prepare to disappear
To seek much warmer climes than ours.
When asters, latest of our summer flowers
Give stained-glass colours to the gardens
Where, dew-spangled webs of spiders glisten in frosty air.
When in the woods the fires of autumn burn
As beech trees, from dark green to amber turn
And other trees their fiery colours show.
Leaves fade to brown and fall, littering below
The woodland ways, to crunch beneath our feet.
In hedge and ditch the brambles black and sweet
Hang lustrous down, waiting for us to pick
Helped by our old and trusty walking stick.
Autumn's a tapestry woven in colours fine,
Until at last they fade in slow decline
And vanish, one by one as the year ages slow
And sees its end beneath the winter's snow.

Margaret B Baguley

The Autumn Air

The sighing owl
Echoes on the
Night air
Impenetrable as
Your eyes,
Black as your hair.

The fox, silent
As a ghost
Trails the edges
Of the wood
Searching for
His lair.
And the cubs
That stir and
Whimper in their
Dreamless sleep
Softly breathe
The autumn air.

Josephine Thomas

AUTUMNAL REFLECTIONS

The sultry days of summer slowly come to a close
As the warm soothing rays of sunshine wane
Veiled by the mists and cool autumn weather
Eclipsed by rich colours of trees all aflame.
All in abundance, berries, fruits, nuts and haws
Preparation for winter is clearly at hand
As bountiful harvests are gathered and stored
Expectations nurtured far across the land.
Whitethroat and Warbler, Redstart and Swift
Make ready for their journey of migration
As frog and hedgehog, bat and dormouse
Seek safe shelter for hibernation.
A season of colour, a joy to behold
A story of survival that is forever retold.

Liam Heaney

Autumn Leaves

I once complained to my guardian, I hated collecting leaves
The same that fell in thousands from off autumnal trees
The way they scattered everywhere, an eyesore on the grass
Like measles on the Earth's own skin, they came down thick and fast

I never thought he'd whisper me about such mundane things
A pet-hate hardly worth the time it took to shrug his wings
Imagine then you my surprise when he did whisper, 'Wait!'
And gave a little lesson me about those leaves I hate

'Look the tree . . . imagine and think the sap inside
As being the very gift of life, it gives the leaf outside
Now think the leaves as people and the seasons as life's span
Made by Him, The Tree of Life, to thrive as best they can

Now muse you but a single leaf from the promise in the bud
To the joy that sees it spread to play its part upon the wood
From its promise in the springtime to the summer's gentle sun
In the wind and rain and frosty morns, that sees the seasons run

And yet, many will fall early, some soon while others late
But all the leaves will see that day they fall . . . it is their fate
And then it is you gather them, till all are cleared away
And the Tree stands bare and skeletal upon a winter's day

Now think the leaves as scattered souls and your gathering as a prayer
To harvest souls who are un-prayed, forlorn, left lying there
For know in all Creation, there's reason and there's why
Those leaves you hate to gather up fall from the Tree and die'

My guardian whispered in my ear, 'Gather them and pray
Think every leaf you gather up as a soul in need that day
By diligence leave none to chance, do your work and with care
And think on them who suffer yet, all for the want of prayer'

Across my face is found a smile, now autumn brings its leaves
For me to concentrate my task, pray un-prayed souls their needs
For love is ere the measure, once He a soul does call
And winter sees my judgement day, when like a life, I fall

M J Banasko

AUTUMN

Grey autumn days press into my soul.
Its dampness pervades every crevice of my being -
With its mouldering leaves shuffled by the wind.

Slumped brown bracken signals a season's ending . . .
Forlorn sheep munch at yellowing grass.
Old man's beard droops wistfully over faded shrubs.

Suddenly!
Stabbing rays of sun shoot through the trees;
My soul leaps at this vivid transformation;
The deadness - a temporary reprieve.

The descending mist returns, silencing
the quick.

This seasonal equinox heralds melancholic
drawing in.

Pam Cole

Autumn

All the leaves
Lay on the ground,
All different colours,
Red, yellow and brown.

All the leaves under my feet
Sound like a million crisps,
All those hot summer days
I really miss.

I come up the path
And through the gate,
Jump into bed
And hibernate.

I curl up in a ball,
Full of fear,
Wake me up,
When spring is here.

Amy Hempstead (12)

AUTUMNAL THOUGHTS

Now autumn drags her russet veil
Over hilltop, woods and lowly dale,
Carelessly erasing all colours bright,
Hiding greenery and summer light.

There's a chill in the air when mists lie low,
Leaves flutter down, as cool winds blow,
Apples ripen on trees while petals fall,
Winter's gloom awaits to enslave us all.

Morning dew glitters on the ground,
Shivering air seems to hover around.
Days shorten while nights become long,
Nature begins her melancholy song.

Autumn shrouds summer's carefree bliss,
Killing the warmth with a deadly kiss.
Sunbathing days are left behind,
Nature's become more cruel and unkind.

The end of the year looms all too near
With its questions for all, so loud and clear:
How many hours have we wasted each day?
Is peace any nearer or further away?

Sheila J Dodwell

ATHENS, AUTUMN

On the sloping streets of Plaka,
summer sags like a yellow balloon
seeping helium in the heat,
tied to a waiting sidewalk chair.

It's hard to tell that north, a month ago,
the snow established its inclemency.
Here, in the purlieu of the Parthenon,
figs and grapes insist that summer stay.

Then above the Agora and iris-blue Aegean,
morning rain becomes a river, rapids, waterfalls,
scouring antique stones and stairs, bringing death
to humble worms and small unseeing things.

Bruised jasmine, the last innocent opium,
curls its scent through rain rung air,
quenching, for a moment, the desire
that strangles us all, for perfection.

Sunday dawn. Asleep. A still-warm room.
Slow, small staccato drumbeats.
Then rain-sodden sheets.
Awake, we revel in the storm-sprung fall.

Marcia M Servente

HIGHLAND AUTUMN

Close of summer with the crisp morning's exuberance
Snow-capped mountains, shimmering iced water in an instance
Colours red to purple and golden, all such extravagance
The richness, Mother Earth holds in abundance.

A deer, deep in the thicket, lies fawning
While a superior stag, high on a Grag, in splendour frowning
Hillsides covered with the rowan and ash, the sunrise crowning
The views so stunning, melts the heart of this autumn dawning.

By the ridge of the forest, leans a rickety farmhouse
Lightly waving wheatfields, lives the family dormouse
Which in return, a scream is heard from the farmer's spouse
Ready to become - game! Lined up in two's are braces of grouse.

Whisky in the distillery! Vats brewing to satisfaction,
Guides showing visitors round, a sense of smells and fascination
Highland cattle toys - toffee and fudge bought in a carton
Also Shetland woollens, kilts and ties made from different tartan.

Above the skies are empty, no sound as autumn came birds migrated
Winter approaching as the snow follows, the community is isolated
Treasured and loved with sheer delight is our icon
Nests high above, in the Caledonian pines, home to the falcon.

Wild animals groom and have a look as they pamper,
Squirrels hiding their winter store, up in the trees they scamper
Hares in coats of white not to be seen, pheasants tiptoe, so nimble
All is set for wintertime - creatures snug and warm as a thimble.

Jan Ross

AUTUMN SHARED

We shall as poets, share with all,
That magic time oft' known as fall.
Where we will celebrate with words,
The parting of the leaves and birds.

The coming of the frosted morn,
The naked trees with foliage shorn.
The dark'ning nights that most embrace,
Sat by as fires warm their place.

As outside, rising winds take hold,
The leaves so brightly coloured, bold
To lay them in a crusty pile,
That when we scatter makes us smile.

Sid 'de' Knees

ORIENTATIONS

A kaleidoscope of orchestrated
images of wild geese klaxons
heralding pilgrimage

embroidering a pattern
of delicate lace designated
co-ordinates converge in space

time entwined in a dream
of receding sights its perils
unfathomed by failing lights

genetics demand the coupling
dance confounding equations
of fanciful chance

the gambled hope
of causality negated
by fumbled uncertainty

habitat achieved by the energy
of survival each species
selected despite human denial

the way ahead by logical
intuitions locks unlocked
revealing false illusions

the insane fear of facing
the self within an innocence
beyond the grasp of reason

life is a mist of soaring
contradictions skybound delays
by headwind interventions

the spearhead alliance
winged by instinct
to a direction ordained.

Michael Fenton

Autumn Days

Oak leaves spiralling to the ground,
Whilst blustery winds blow round and round.
Leaves changing into russets and gold,
Herald's a season that's large and bold.

Conkers are falling off the horse-chestnut tree,
With plenty there for you and me.
Threading them through on to a string
May make other boys sit up and grin

Scrunching the fallen leaves underfoot,
And the acorns we picked up as if they were loot,
The harvest festival in church was due,
And we packed boxes and goodies right next to the pew

The roses around us were wilting fast,
And as their beauty faded our sorrow was vast.
Not much colour in the garden now,
Especially as the wind blows and how.

The autumn rains are heavy and strong,
And any new gardener can go wrong.
You must know when to plant your seed,
To be first in the spring to reap your crop.

Late holidays should be taken soon,
As hotels are fully booked with little room,
Winter seems to be crowding in,
As we wait for the first flutter of snow to begin.

G Nutbeem

Autumn

Falling, tumbling, twisting, turning,
Leaves faded green and tawny-golden,
Ochre, amber, shapes distorted,
Form a carpet 'neath the woodland.

Hedgerows, fruit trees, heavy laden
With the bounties of the summer,
Crimson, amethyst and emerald,
Fleshy spheres for winter food.

Nuts on hazel, velvet tipped,
Acorns silken cupped in green,
Chestnuts fallen, sheathed in prickles,
Walnuts' wrinkled surface bared.

Spiders busy spinning, weaving,
Unsuspected traps for insects,
Catch the dewdrops, beadlike, jewels,
Veils with pearliest threads the meadows.

Soldier-drilled the gathering swallows,
Practice runs from early morn'.
Twitters, chatting all excited,
Maiden flights soon to begin.

Resident robin stays behind,
Curiously watching worm, exposed,
Trills, his chest expanding proudly,
Left the guardian of the garden.

Starkly black and brown the branches,
Turning into dead and dank,
Winter lurking in the shadows,
Grasps with freezing fingers furled.

Jean Bagshaw

My Parallel Autumn

Natures beautiful autumn returns every year,
Is autumn for humans something to fear?
Winter must follow but we cannot tell
If we will survive to share it as well.

Autumn has colours in leaves and in grasses
My sight becomes dimmer - I'll have to wear glasses
Hibernation begins as every one knows
Hang on a minute, I must have a doze.

The autumn mists take longer in clearing
No birds are singing - am I hard of hearing?
The sun in the sky gets lower and lower,
My senses get dull, my movements are slower.

Some beautiful trees will lose every leaf
I'll follow suit, start loosing my teeth.
Days will grow shorter with evenings that chill
Should sort out my life, must make out a Will.

Birds will migrate, the tern, swift and swallow
I'd like to feel warmer, wish I could follow,
They leave winter's snow with never a care,
I can't escape, get snowy white hair.

The beauty of autumn, it will not last,
Winter will follow when it is past,
Then spring and summer will come again,
I'll only know winter, God what is that pain?

The harvest in autumn is all gathered in
Did I have a good life? How much did I sin?
The winter time now gets deeper and deeper,
My life's at an end, next comes the Grim Reaper!

Kenneth L Tropman

WASPISH

Their entry was uncovered
On the day she trimmed the ivy
And upset the settlers
In her roof-space.
Puzzling how they fit in God's great scheme of things
She watched enthralled, appalled,
The busy to-and-fro
To satisfy their queen,
Fecundant in her Chinese paper lampshade.
Picnic spoilers,
Ice cream pests,
Annoying stings on wings.

That night she crept, thief-like,
And squirted poison in the hole.

At dawn she hurried out . . .
And still the wasps flew back and forth
Between the ivy leaves.
But now, when each one left the nest,
It stumbled, fell,
Before regaining flight,
Each body with a small, white bomb,
Egg-heavy.

Tirelessly, all through the day, the workers hastened,
Single-minded, sacrificial,
To remove their precious future
To a place of safety

And the woman watched
Ashamed.

Dee Yates

Autumn

When the autumn leaves are falling
And the days are drawing in
I hear the voice of my wife calling
It's time for you to come in.
You are tired having worked all day
Clearing the garden ready
To plant flowers to bloom in May
Making sure they are steady
The day ends with the setting sun
The night air begins to cool
To sit down and just enjoy one
Glass of wine, what I'm no fool
At night the leaves are still falling
Falling from the trees so proud
On them the moon is still shining
Clear blue skies without a cloud
Autumn, the time I enjoy most
Countryside full of colour
The squirrel on the garden post
The robins tame as ever.

L R Jennings

THE LEAVES START TO FALL

The leaves are all different shades of brown
It is time for them to journey slowly to the ground
A slight breeze may come and off they go
Swaying to and fro in the wind they flow

Autumn has come and things all change
The trees in their glory now start to look strange
What becomes of the leaves so green
All different shades magnificent to be seen

A whistle in the wind will suddenly appear
Dark cold nights, some filled with fear
The animals hunt around for their winter store
Some are not seen for a few weeks or more

Oh autumn must you come so quick and so fast
Why has summer to go, can we not make it last
Dark nights and rain, do we not have a choice
If we must, we will shout for summer with a strong voice

The seasons come and they pass without any say
All we do is take whatever comes on this day
Autumn, autumn, please come and go
Give us back the summer days we love and know

Cynthia Scott

THOUGHTS OF AUTUMN

I always know when autumn comes
For the Rose Bay fairies fly,
Time to look forward to harvest
The long summer days have flown by,
Rosy red hips of the wild rose
The sensation of misty morns,
And walking along by the hedgerows
Where we spy the red haws of hawthorn.
The swifts have already departed
The swallows they will migrate soon,
And hedgehogs feed eagerly on slugs
In the light of the harvest moon.
Black fruits of elderberry hang from the tree
The potatoes soon to be lifted,
From rich earth where they have spent summer
Which from it they will have to be sifted.
The buzzing of wasps in drunken flight
Their flying time will now not be long,
Whilst the logs are cut by the chainsaw
Which makes its peculiar song.
Time now to lift blooms of the summer
Which have given us such delight,
A time to plant bulbs for the springtime
Which will give us a joyful sight.
Leaves swirl downward from the trees
Spurred on by autumn gales,
The clear night skies of late autumn
Will bring frosts as hard as nails.
Autumn, the season of Advent
When we prepare for the birth of a child.

David A Garside

FALLEN LEAVES

Autumn leaves are falling all around,
Parchment dry, crisp and yellow,
Lying like my dreams on hard ground,
I've been deserted by my fellow.

Wind blown, tree waste in corner pile,
White rima, icing coated leafy waste.
He'd been frosty with me for a while,
Like a scalded cat he took off in haste.

Fallen leaves underfoot, brittle and tattered,
Crunch, as my directionless feet wandered
Days past like pages of life's book scattered,
Torn free, strewn, time wasted and squandered.

Russet and golden mantle trees are shedding,
Cycle of life, circle of renewal,
Marriage rings, planning for our wedding
My future suddenly barren, so cruel.

From nature's decay will come regeneration
Spring will bring blossom and leaf bud
New dreams ready to emerge from degradation
Older, wiser, stronger, seasoned like wood.

Patricia Susan Dixon MacArthur

AUTUMN

Feather light leaves float gently to the ground.
Flakes of red and yellow, golden brown.
Fat and juicy blackberries abound
In hedges, ripened by the weakening sun.
The atmosphere is chilly. Summer's done.
Apples, luscious plums, weigh down their trees
Home-grown tomatoes, courgettes, beans and peas,
For making jams and stews to eat or freeze.
Abundance now but everything is dying.
It's winter next and time it is a-flying.

>There's melancholy in the air,
>A mourning for the passing year.
>A feel of 'Here we are again'
>A sadness one can't quite explain.

Flowers fading, leaving dead remains.
Dampness, fogs and mist and heavy rains
That fill the dykes, the gullies and the drains.
Early frost and gardens, wet with dew.
Aches and pains and coughs and colds and flu.
Collect your garden furniture and stack,
Summer clothing you can also pack
Bring out your woollies, hats and gloves and mac.
Evenings long and dreary. Shortened days.
Darkened mornings, tempting one to laze.

>There's melancholy in the air.
>Regrets about the passing year,
>For what's been done, or not been done
>And doubts about what's yet to come.

H Leventhall

AUTUMN JEWELS

When purple flowers have turned to silver
and glisten with the sunshine's rays.
The promise of another season,
comes with the pleasant autumn days.

When golden daisies make a refuge
for black and amber hungry guests
Which soon will turn to red and silver
bright jewels of the autumn days.

When emerald green runs riot over
neglected parts of garden ways.
From common - tortoiseshell appears
to drift on sunny autumn days.

Wesley Stephens

INSTRUMENT FOR WAR GAMING

Now is the time of year when children busily
hurl sticks dizzily
skywards,
not knowing what may fall.

Arching towards their apogee, momentarily
they hang there in mid air
before
gravity guided,
they boomerang downwards
through bosky canopy ricocheting,
raping.

Within bole-encircling subfusc shade earth
is met with velvet thump

Here, joining jetsam of their own origin,
snapped stems, lacerated leaves,
and other dross,
the tree's loss,
they lie in nadir's nimbus
amid strewn nexus of wanton wastefulness,
advancing nature's clock

Boys surge, stoop, sift feverishly for possession.

Casket, green as tree frog and soon breached,
betrays a confidence, revealing within
its germinal form, coddled as its yolk
and wondrous to behold.
Mahogany mellow, silk slippery
and profoundly polished as Cremona viol!
Paragon for any craftsman taking pride
in immaculate conclusion.

But lustre is transitory, perfection fades
and seedy travesty is strung for tournament,
a thing of beauty becoming an instrument
for war gaming.

Kelvin Carter

EVENING SILENCES

September evening, walk up the hill
In distance, grey silhouettes of hills reaching down to the Bay.
The evening light shimmers on the Bay waters.
Traffic as if like Dinky toys rushing home on the black tarmac roads
But nothing is heard of the busy bustle on the hill
A black and white crocodile line against the green hedges as the bovine
Ladies wend their way back to the fields after another milking
God's faithful church and acre in silent expectancy wait
for the beloved to return
But of the ancient trees, they are so quiet
A field of rams, all boys together crop grass and keep watch in silence
Two hooded crows sit atop a telegraph pole,
basking in the late evening sunshine
Conspirators both silently watch being watched
A smoky garden bonfire fills the still air with scent that clings
to clothes and remains
Swallows swoop in the quietness before dark, catching their last meal
of the day on the wing
Succulent blackberries vie in the hedgerow with gramophone coned
flowers of white convulvalus
Miss H calls for her tame pheasant, her shrill voice carrying tenderness
and concern into her silent garden
I turn for home in the silence save for a mournful cronk of a lone crow
winging himself homeward

Hilary Jean Clark

NOVEMBER

Leafy pathways indicate
That autumn has arrived
Trees are shedding leaves
Of every shape and size

Harvest has been gathered
Fields now take a rest
The countryside no longer, is at its very best.

Foggy damp mornings
No sun to shed its light
November days seem almost - like night.

Soon it will be Christmas
A special time of year
Which helps to spell the winter gloom
And fill our hearts with cheer.

Christine Hardemon

The Drawing In

Autumn is an artist's paradise
Of many tints and hues and shades
That mellow as the afternoon sun fades
And gathers round the leafy glades.

That chill of air that fills the dawning
And proceeds throughout the morning.
The falling light that now comes early
And darkens into deepest night
Encourages us moreover to sleep so tight.

Sheila Lewis

NOVEMBER FALLS

How clear in sleep a mind recalls
November falls from harbour walls,
dumb concrete boots and splashing sounds,
dead flower wreaths float sickly
sweet halos slowly drowning.

Confused by red and blue regrets
the sun then sets, spent cigarettes
flicked nonchalant to watery graves,
old love affairs mount spiral
stairs leading steeply downward.

Stolen on a breath that sighs,
fake alibis at crying eyes,
gasping hooks and dragging dreams
way out to sea where they may
be consigned to sleep with fishes.

With grim resign a mind recalls
November falls when winter calls
with spells of ice from frosted tongues,
the iron bind, the lemming love,
blind suicides of virgins.

Tony Bush

AUTUMANIA

When leaves start falling in the autumn days
And birds are grouping to fly away,
The shortening days and lengthening nights
With winds getting stronger, too strong to fly kites.
Sometimes there's a fog too thick to see through,
Then we are left wondering just what we can do.

Hedgehogs and others will hibernate now,
They've had a long summer, but they know how
To take care of themselves during these colder days,
They'll just lie asleep in their survival phase.
When they wake up, all refreshed, full of life
Once more, they will look for a wife.

The leaves are brown and crackly
They're lying underfoot,
Instead of hanging on the trees
Where they were originally put.
They've died and fallen to the ground,
They fell without a sound.

The marvellous colours of an autumn sky
Creep gracefully o'er the world.
As we glance up to this wonderful scene
We think, to ourselves, has this always been?
Has God made this? This enchanting sight
That stretches before us after the night?

When autumn leaves us, regretfully behind,
With thoughts we will cherish
In our thinking mind,
Of colourful leaf falls and fog in the air.
We'll ponder on these things
And say, 'The world's fair!'

W Thirkettle

. . . INTO THE WIND YOU GO

When there's no wind to carry you
on, you stumble and fall.

Beneath the oak tree you fall,
floating through the air by the
swift autumn breeze.

Until you land on the crisp grass
surrounded by yourself, yet you drag
your feet along the untouched ground.

Until you find a sheltered spot to
cast away your last breath . . .
. . . into the wind you go.

Gemma Mountain

WHEN DANCING BLAZE SUBSIDES

The year is closing in as days
Begin to shrink. Their lives the same,
As still advancing dusk precedes
The laggard dawn: as softer light
At noon allows a gentler way
Than when the fires of youth consumed
Their thoughts with passion's fickle flames.
The gaudy dress of summer's put
Away. The muted garb she wears
To ward from cold conceals what sun
Revealed and lustful eye revered.
But now attention turns to eyes.
At last he sees the person she
Has screened from world - a loving gift
To those for whom she cares. And so
He starts to learn to know her heart,
And thus begins to feel her warmth,
To cherish what she really is.
It's when the dancing blaze subsides
The glowing coals confer a peace,
Allowing silent thanks a chance,
Inviting quiet forgiving kiss.

Henry Disney

AUTUMN'S HARBINGER

So it's the end of July
Too bright the sun, too long
Seared the earth, sapped am I of strength
Come sweet rain, torrents at night, I'll lie and listen to your song

Why is the summer so intense?
We moan at the mention of a shower
But come fairy rain, linger long we welcome you
Refresh the wilting flower

In terms of time twill not be long
Before comes my favourite mellow season's splash
For today I saw across the way
In full red berried glory - the mountain ash.

Barbara Robson

TO AUTUMN

Autumn the final season of the year,
ascended on us today.
The leaves have started to fall,
before they even turn a golden hue.

Everything is so early now,
is this due to global warming?
The leaves once turned to red and gold;
but lack of rain has left the earth so dry.

Flowers and plants so beautiful a month ago,
are suddenly drooping and slowly dying;
the nights draw in so quickly,
I settle myself by the fire.

I think of days gone by,
a glorious warming summer;
the fields have now been harvested,
all is safely gathered in.

Food is there for another winter, all is well.
I settle down to have my drink,
and scan my Christmas present list.

And I think of another day,
tomorrow I start to clear the leaves.

Janet Cavill

AUTUMN

Autumn is a delightful time
The coloured trees are so divine.
With leaves of multi marbled shades
Parading proudly in the glades.
Mountain ash and rowan too
With berries red, a different hue
Various greens adorned with dew
A magical scene, spectacular view.
Uplifting our souls in awe and wonder
A time to appreciate and ponder
God's creation knows no bounds
Take your time and look around
Walking home to the church bell sound
Just time for a cuppa, before singing out loud.

Dorothy Squires

Autumn Leaves

They look so sad those fallen leaves
    crumpled, bruised and dead,
Torn from bare uncaring trees
    to lie neglected on their earthy bed,
Once they were the colours on
    nature's seasonal dresses,
Hanging like clinging tassels
    to her softly shimmering tresses.

Leaves which once hid songbirds
    from their enemies all around,
Gave shelter to weary travellers
    walking beneath them on the ground,
They cradled perfumed blossoms
    from which grew nature's seeds,
To ensure that we of human kind
    could satisfy a human's needs.

Some were golden, brightly tinted,
    others were russet red,
Now crunching brittle underfoot,
    all are sear and withered,
Swept by the brush of whipping wind,
    and lashed by pitiless rain,
'Tis nature's way of telling us . . .
    that autumn has come again.

F R Smith

Autumn's Past

The bright green leaves have turned to gold
The cuckoos long since gone
The golden fall has come at last
As the year journeys on.

Autumn is a lovely time, beauty is everywhere
But like a quiet calm evening it seems a time to care
A time to think of beauty before dark winter comes
To rest and think before dark days are come.

The year grows older and moves on but it is ever fair
The lovely evening sunset the gentle fall of leaves
There's such a blessed calm so wonderful it seems.

We live through spring and summer
The golden autumn's gone
Winter fast draws on me as time moves swiftly on.

But as I reach my twilight years
I think back with a smile
And perhaps I shed some silent tears
My autumn's gone awhile
But I can still think back and love
The seasons long since gone
And thank my blessed Lord above
Who let me carry on.

C E Growcott

CESSATION

That autumn day, the sun in flight
Did terminate the lucent day-long light.
A cold and bare-bleak wind now clipped
And redly-orange foliate stripped
Protesting branches waving high for aid
That dusty prismatic colours would not fade.
The coming weather, heedless harsh and cruel
Will ne'er depart from this exacting rule,
That all must perish - lost their beauty bright
Before the winter solstice in full flight.
So may it drive me always onward too
No shortened stride nor even backwards view,
Accept what melancholy now awaits
And hope my spring 'tends waiting at her gates.

Sarah Blackmore

Autumn

Autumn is my time of the year,
The heat of summer on the wane
And darker nights, which I prefer.
The landscape softer and more pleasing.
I like the fresher mornings.
The brisker air
And ploughed fields under a blue sky.

Heatwaves are not for me.
Too stultifying by far
And draining one of energy.
That's when I long for autumn.

September is on the edge of winter.
The sun is kind and gentle on the skin.
Though nights can be cold,
But this I do not mind.
Yes, autumn is the time for me.

Brenda Lismer

AUTUMN...

Autumn heralds colours the like of which is so hard to tell
Stripy leaves and brown leaves just lying where they fell
Reds and yellows and orange leaves to name but a few
A dozen different kinds of greens adorn the trees in view

Trees once with leafy dresses now naked but unbowed
Their coats of many colours have abandoned them for now
Still haughty in their nakedness but shy beyond compare
Standing by in silence planning new dresses for next year

The gallant horse chestnut about to drop his conker fruit
He is also looking forward to his next year's brand new suit
The sycamore once more expels her little helicopter seeds
They whirl and swirl and land then just vanish in the weeds

Virginia is a creeper who drapes her limbs along my roof
Resplendent in her summer green so proud and so aloof
Overnight she'll slip into her robe of vibrant stunning red
Feast your eyes upon her now before her cloak she sheds

Autumn is a time that starts the magic winter hibernation
The days grow short, the dark nights are of long duration
The hedgehog hides himself away safe from all around
So pleased with the new straw bed he accidentally found

Lighting early evening fires to keep chilling winds at bay
Heard it on the radio that the first snow's not so far away
While the weather does its worst, one thing is for certain
If the winter snow is a blanket then the autumn is a curtain

When the curtains open up and the blanket back is thrown
If you look very carefully you will see the making of new gowns
The mighty oak has tiny shoots and the pretty hedgerows too
For him a cloak of Sherwood green to grace his limbs anew

Like the colours of a rainbow autumn flaunts her many hues
A glorious, fabulous wardrobe beneath a cape of many blues
Winter, spring and summer are seasons that we so welcome
But none so much as the cornucopia that comes with autumn.

Ceejay

Autumn

Pack away the lady painted
Great oak leaves now fallen tainted
The scent of flower on evening air
Has left late summer's cooling fayre
Gold brown raiment on dormant trees
Is wrest from twig by autumn breeze
Geese fly south in lines pre-set
A route their goslings can't forget
The rutt begins and stags will fight
By a scream of vixens in the night
A cold sun dies on a cobalt sky
As a squirrel sleeps on nuts put by
The badger setts to wait the spring
Yet the robin has a song to sing
Shadows long the days grow short
As winter follows this cohort.

J P Worthy

Autumn

It was September in beautiful New England
My first hurricane
The wonderful scenery, the beautiful trees
How you remember

Bill was at work
The sky was getting darker and darker

It was very quiet
Before the storm
Then the wind swirling so loud
I looked at our tiny daughter
In all the noise she looked so small
Then Bill arrived, was I glad
I calmed down and pretended I had not
Been worried at all.

Phyllis O'Connell

AUTUMN BLUES

Oh! No it's September,
The month ends in ember,
September, October, well November, December,
Christmas oh dear!
The feelings I get this time of year.

It's a pleasant day really,
With late summer sun,
This month is quite nice as a rule,
An Indian summer would please everyone,
But kids have gone back to school.

It's quite autumnal today,
The combine harvesters have been put away,
Already the fields are under the plough,
And plump, ripe, blackberries hang on the bough.

Winter's coming, the signs are there,
Like bookings taken for your Christmas fayre.
Decorations and tinsel in our local store,
I may book up for a Mediterranean tour.

The golden rods are dying,
We've had a bit of a drought,
The garden looks quite tatty,
And needs some sorting out.
Wind falls on the lawn, potatoes by the sack,
Don't forget tomorrow, the clocks are turning back.

Ken Rolfe

SEPTEMBER'S LEGACY

Amid tranquil days and meaner nights
when migrant birds prepare for flight,
dawn sleeps later every day
and dusk is never far away.

Days of summer's glory linger,
overgrown and over-burdened
with such a luscious store.

Wasps feed voraciously as though aware
of an unseen danger.
They fall, stupefied and angry.
The sting in the tail of the mellow season.

Unlike the brief morning lick of summer,
autumn's dew clings as if to warn
of the need to wear stouter shoes or boots.

The electric blanket, shunned all summer long,
suddenly becomes a coveted, comforting companion.

Soon, General Heating
will assemble his troops in every room.
Although an essential safeguard,
they are viewed with disdain.
Their pay will certainly rise again this year.

They will remain at their post until well into the spring.
Slowly but surely eating away at the precious stockpile,
carefully laid on one side to pay for the summer holiday.

Kinsman Clive

A Poem For Autumn

I love the autumn; I love the colour of the leaves
I love the gold and the russet and the yellow and the brown:
I love the green that hangs on till the bitter end
When the cruel November frost finally wins the battle,
And all, but a few, lie dying on the ground.
But the mighty trees, though naked, are merely sleeping
And will wake again next spring.

I love the autumn; I was born in that season,
In September when the fruits are mellow and the sunset's golden.
When gentle winds swirl the fallen leaves around,
                                  chasing them into corners.
Children in the park run and kick the leaves
                    from their tidy hiding places.
When swans and geese noisily migrate to warmer climes,
And lights are lit early on buses and trains, in shops and homes.
The autumn brings a feeling of peace; I love the autumn.

Sandra Benson

SHADES OF AUTUMN

Nature casts off her summer gowns
To lay a carpet of green and gold
Dancing branches sway
As winter's icy breath blows through
Scarecrow trees.

A leaden canopy of woollen clouds
Covers the earth with sulky tears
Moody winds moan as they sweep
Across the changing season.

Phoebe casts a shadowy light upon
A winter darkened land
Earth shall sleep until awakened
In the morning of rebirth.

Carole Harradence

AUTUMN LEAVES

From bud to flourishing leaf
Fully grown leaves shelter animals and plants beneath
As summer ends trees start to fade
Green leaves gradually change from day to day.
Approaching autumn, the days get cooler
For deciduous trees there is less available water.
Leaves turn red and gold, glowing and bright
The vibrant colours are a magnificent sight
Caught in the sun's rays the trees are full of beauty
Radiant, outstanding in all their glory
When the leaves dry out and turn to brown
Gently they fall and float to the ground.
The autumn leaves crunch beneath our feet
Get blown into drifts in abandoned heaps
In wind and rain leaves are trampled and flattened
The beautiful autumn leaves, discarded, forgotten.

Lorna June Burdon

AUTUMN TIME

Autumn is the time of year
When everything gets ready,
For the winter's months.
The trees changing colours
With leaves, reds, coppers and yellows
Which keep on falling to the ground
Gardens too have their show of colours,
With their summer flowers
Before Jack Frost comes along
And cuts them all down.
Also, the stillness that comes too,
When birds have gone to warmer countries,
And the nip in the air
Tells us that autumn is here.

A F Hiscocks

ELEMENTS

When summer's gone,
People around you say, 'Soon Christmas.'

What is going on?
The sky stays blue forever,

But everything else linked with the earth,
Is fading into this rusty but rather nice tone,

Renewing their coat for the next season,
The trees are similar to fashion designer,

Colourful from the first day,
To the last minute of the show,

Therefore, if the shape is identical,
At least, the range of colour has to be original.

Laurent Rickling

IT'S AUTUMN-ATIC!

The heatwave's gone! The sun retreats!
The summer bids adieu!
'What a scorcher!' thus completes
The season known as 'Phew!'
It's 'autumn-atic' what ensues
And winter waits its turn . . .
September starts its coloured hues
On trees as green as fern.
Is that a chill within the bones?
Rheumatic pains increase.
Across the nation, hear the groans
From those who can't find peace!
So on with extra togs on beds,
Our duvets to improve.
So on with extra logs from sheds,
Our living rooms to soothe.
The folks with central heating, too,
Turn up a notch each night.
It's no good if their feet turn blue,
Cos that would be a sight!
Out come the extra pairs of socks,
The mittens and the scarves!
And soon we have to change the clocks -
We don't do things by halves!
We watch the roads in case of ice!
We watch dark days take hold!
Then chestnuts ripen in a trice -
All shiny, good as gold!
Then Hallowe'en's bewitching spell
Enchants, once cast, till past . . .
Bonfires burn as if from Hell!
Then Christmas comes - *at last!*

Denis Martindale

MIXED FEELINGS

Summertime in Paris . . .
Sights, sounds, smells
Hustle, bustle,
A sea of smiling faces,
Happy conversations,
Pavement cafés,
Wine and dine
Or just pass the time.

Back home again,
Children return to school,
Prepare the family meal.
Autumn brings a mixture of feelings . . .
A little uncertain,
A little unsure.
Winter approaches . . .
Wind, rain and snow.

Practise the piano or guitar,
What was that tune?
A ray of sunshine brightens the gloom,
Settle down to a routine,
Join an evening class or two,
Time to start something new!

Cathy Mearman

AUTUMN

Summer is gone,
Autumn is here.
The nights are dark,
The time is near.
It's back to school,
For hard working days.
No time to laugh,
No time to play.
The leaves all start to patter and fall,
The animals hide.
But that's not all,
They're hibernating.
They're getting their food,
There's no time to lay in.
Autumn has come it's time for some changes,
The world revolves, revolves and arranges.

Sheun Oshinbolu (11)

FIVE MORE MINUTES

The mornings come so soon,
Just five more minutes in bed.
The duvet feels so snug and warm,
I'd like to stay here instead.

We shuffle to work in the cold,
Get damp to our bones in the rain.
All day long we think of home,
When we can be back in our warm cosy bed.

Nikki Healey

SAD

A longing for
sun-kissed cheeks,
balmy heat,
a kaleidoscope of vibrant colour,
sunny smiles, warm hearts
and generous minds.

Instead of
being SAD,
the dark evenings,
the chill in the air.
Heads down, eyes averted,
rushing home to get out
of the cold.

'Cheer up. It could be worse.'
Could be worse?
It will get worse.
Leaves will divorce the trees.
The seeping cold will challenge
us mere mortals.

Hallowe'en, Guy Fawkes night,
Christmas and snow will be
the prizes on offer
for persevering through autumn.
But will it cure the SADness?
No. Only a prescription for the return
of summer will be the guaranteed treatment.

Naomi Donegan

MOTHER NATURE

The gloom of that late autumn, the stars passing by
on velvet coloured background. Cold, dark and endless sky.

My lonely, empty balcony
The silence
The memory
of a lost summer
The memories of you and me.

A view of an empty magpie nest
leaves are falling.
Mother Nature needs her rest.

Minutes, hours, weeks and months - they fly
Another season - another year is passing by.

Peaceful, dark embrace
Late autumn
Another wrinkle in my face
This mighty world we're in
what a mysterious race.

Autumn, colourful. My hands are cold
Life is passing. I'm feeling old.

Cascades of autumn leaves. Slowly by the wind they're spread
The colours Mother Nature gives - symphonies of orange, yellow, red.

Time for reflections. Being apart
wondering . . .
Waiting, knowing this is the start
of months of longing
for another spring
to make me young and wild at heart.

The peaceful, dark violet, blackish-blue
The stars passing by. I will wait for you . . .

Jorunn Ingebrigtsen

DIFFERENT COLOURS

Autumn is approaching very fast
Soon the summer will be behind in the past,
The leaves on bushes and trees will change colour
Making them look much brighter not duller.
Enjoy all the different colours as they change
From yellows to browns it is wonderful range,
Then the leaves will be falling on the ground,
When dry they make a loud crunching sound.
But when wet and lying on the floor there
Beware they can be very slippery so take care,
Some may go as compost while others go on a bonfire
But whatever use you make of them it's your desire.
Just enjoy the wonderful and colourful scene
As the bushes and trees lose their bright green,
Once a year the autumn season comes around
Enjoy it once more before the leaves fall to ground,
And just as each season must come to a close
I will close now before it snows.

George Reed

Autumn

Autumn is a wonderful time of year
With the heat of the summer over and winter drawing near
The leaves are changing colour to red, yellow and brown too
Trees are shedding a pathway for all to tramp through.

The lambs are missing they gambol no more
No doubt glad to be undercover and warm that's for sure
There are crops to be harvested before winter sets in
The farmer has so much to do - it puts him in a spin.

Time is approaching when curtains need to be drawn
No more time to spend gardening - or mowing the lawn
Lights in the houses for all to see
Not much else to do so we watch TV.

Still autumn is such a beautiful season we all agree
And will be with us till eternity.

Marjorie Ridley

AUTUMN TIME

The scythe that cut the corn lies idle now
The fields of stubble wait the autumn plough
The farmer rests his weary limbs, the harvest's in
The country housewife gathers wool, begins to spin.

Thus another year comes to its close
I see the falling leaves, the dying rose
I note the early fading light, the evening chills
Morning frosts now glisten on distant hills.

The trees are all leaf stripped and bare
Their fallen leaves wind scattered everywhere
Early morning mist rolls slowly o'er the fields
Summer's gone and nature to the coming winter yields.

Soon the hedgerows will be glistening with frost
Till comes a weakling sun when it is lost
To leave them decked with dripping pearls
As day by day winter's coat unfurls.

'Tis time to huddle round the fire
The wind is keener and the air is drier
Time to think of Christmas pudding and mince pies
Look to the new year as the old one dies.

H H Steventon

AUTUMN... IS IT GOOD OR BAD?

A gentle breeze stirring in the air . . .
A cold wind whirling around me,
Trying to drag me off my feet,
Attempting to snatch away my warm, woollen coat.

Emerald green grass below my feet . . .
A carpet of leaves,
Crunching loudly with every step I take,
Yet, they are so colourful.

Pretty and fragrant flowers in full bloom . . .
Petals spread all over the ground,
Flower heads in tatters,
No more sweet smelling blossoms.

But . . . what about the good things about autumn?

Children dancing merrily around a bonfire,
Fireworks shooting into the sky like rockets,
Sparklers glittering in every hand,
A warm fire to warm up our cold hands and faces.

Hallowe'en pumpkins outside houses,
Trick and treaters all dressed up,
Pendle Hill is the place to be,
That is . . . if you are brave enough!

All that remains for me to ask is:

Autumn . . . good or bad?

Mrinalini Dey

A Touch Of Frost In The Autumn Air

The alchemy of autumn turns to gold
The green of alder, beech and sycamore.
The harvest's in, the stubble landscape rolled
By giant drums of coiled and gilded ore.

The only creature cooing in the woods
An earnest sounding cushet dove,
Late nesting, softly warbling. Could
They but sing the joys of spring, the grove

Would dance to wrens' and robins' song.
But now they pipe a plaintive note,
Wistful, spasmodic, for the year is long
And winter's sadness rises in the throat.

Down from the moorland bracken comes
The bobbing whinchat, black of cheek.
A windfall to decay succumbs.
A harvest mouse declines to squeak.

Norman Bissett

PICTURES IN THE FIRE

Autumn bonfires
Cracking away
As I burn the moulding leaves
Of yesterday.

Throw in the hurts,
The pain, the fear
The grief that assailed me
Throughout the year.

Stand with hot tea
Looking at flames
My mind wanders back
To sunnier days . . .

I stand alone,
The flames are licking
I take your photos
And throw them in . . .

Not a baptism of fire
Rather, a funeral pyre.
The celluloid shrivels up and hisses
I look and wonder but not too much . . .

Just like throwing on spent leaves
On this crisp autumn morning
I've just cleared you out of my closet . . .
No more mourning.

Liz Osmond

TYWARDEATH

As autumn progressed more and more
brown leaves outnumbered the green ones.
So profuse was this conquest it could only end in a bonfire.
The high winds looted the branches for this very purpose
performing them in a vortex circus.
A canopy was now a carpet, a mass grave
on which we all walked.
People talked about Robin Hood and Lincoln green
but brown was all that could be seen.
Each day was darker sooner than the last
and we all longed for greener times.
Millions had cashed in their sap
just to get to the end of the path, swept up in a heap.
They had though one last trick
and that was to light up an autumn night sky,
then say a final goodbye, as ash.

Vann Scytere

AUTUMN'S GLORY

I find I must give thanks anew
For all the rich autumnal glories spread;
For morning mist and gently falling dew
I find I must give thanks anew.
With each leaf that's changing hue
From green to russet, gold, or red,
I find I must give thanks anew
For all the rich autumnal glories spread.

I find I must give thanks again
For the odour of the orchard trees;
For autumn's bounty made so plain
I find I must give thanks again -
Though I can't God's love explain,
It's in experiences like these;
I find I must give thanks again
For the odour of the orchard trees!

Dan Pugh

AUTUMN FESTIVAL

A festival of colour,
A dazzling display
Celebrates the season
In its flamboyant way.

Each day we see a pageant
Of pigments bright and bold -
Technicolour pictures
That constantly unfold.

Autumn is an artist
Giving a master class
In use of tints and textures
No painter could surpass.

His nature is selective
For with restraint and tact
He buffs the copper beeches
But leaves the browns intact.

His two-tone hedges ripple
As sunlight comes and goes
On rose-red hawthorn berries
And satin sable sloes.

Crimson flames and ochre flares
With blaze of gold conspire
To consume the last of green
And set the woods on fire.

Autumn's lavish palette
Can vary with the light,
As brilliant as the dawning
Or pallid as the night.

Celia G Thomas

THE SILENT STILL

The silent still of autumn's days
When all around is mist and haze
That cloaks the trees at dawn's sunrise
To bring delights before our eyes

The scorching heat of summer sun
Is over now, we've just begun
To slow and ponder, walk awhile
Down lanes now quiet - climb a stile

The colours fade from summer glory
To bring about a different story
The leaves are turning russet brown
To fall again, time's winding down

A season of a different bounty
Of fruits and flowers - from every county
The folk that grow, show off their prizes
Which deep love grew, all shapes and sizes

The morns are cool, the nights draw in
And so with us, we look within
To reap the fruits of our deep soul
The thoughts that serve to make us whole

Old thoughts just like the autumn leaves
Fall to make way for new beliefs
Which serve to teach us life's new lessons
We only need to watch the seasons

To trust in winter's deep dark days
Reflect on all we love and praise
And so we freely look at spring
To find the work that makes us sing

Move onto summer's heat and fire
To bring about all we desire
Then autumn comes, we trust let go
And once again fall in the flow.

Gina Bowman

A Reason To Cuddle

I like autumn with the dark nights
And the lack of sunlight
And the breeze around my knees
And the pools of ice
And the days as cold as nights
I like my gloves, my scarf and my ear muffs
I like the sight of lamps lit at night
I like to cuddle and feel the warmth
Of your breath around my neck
I know it's cool, what the heck
Give me warmth like I said
Let's go off to bed
With breakfast to follow
It will be spring tomorrow.

M N Darvil

Autumn Harvest

It is November, and a breaking dawn
Slowly pulls the veil of darkness aside,
Exposing the stark features of late autumn.

Hedges, somewhat overgrown, and trees,
Their branches almost denuded of leaves,
Cast pale shadows across frost-hardened fields.

Hidden beneath furrows of shrivelled shoots,
Clinging in clusters to the buried roots,
Lies a rich legacy of warm summer sun.

Swollen tubers, each pregnant with energy,
Await the arrival of a tractor-drawn digger
To deliver them from their womb of clay.

There to be pirated by a stooping horde
Of teenagers, a mittened laughing crew of recruits,
Delighted to be potato picking out of doors.

Treating the raw cold, and the back breaking toil,
As part of some money-making open air adventure
That just has to be better than the routine of school.

Andrew Farmer

THE SOFT CONTENTED SIGH OF AN AUTUMN BREEZE

The russet rain of autumn gently falls upon the ground.
The silent tears of summer cascading all around.
There is sadness for the passing season, in the falling of the leaves,
But autumn has no thought for why the summer grieves.

The outstretched arms of summer reach imploringly to the sky,
As high above migrating birds in close formation fly.
The shower falls inexorably, slipping from arboreal fingers,
Daylight shrinks with each passing day, as summer no longer lingers.

An air of quiet serenity descends upon the earth,
The season's growth is over, until next spring's rebirth.
For now the arms of Mother Earth reach out in soft embrace,
As summer's swansong dies on the wind,
                      and autumn assumes her place.

A glistening dew hangs all around in the cool fresh morning air,
And diamond studded webs of silk betray a spider's lair.
Rustling in the fallen leaves a squirrel gathers his winter store,
And the insects of the undergrowth tunnel new quarters
                      'neath the forest floor.

The earth sighs in contentment, for the summer's work is done,
And now with the falling russet rain, autumn's time has come.
The forest yawns in readiness for a time to rest is nigh,
And the breeze echoes through the empty boughs,
                      in a soft contented sigh . . .

Brian L Porter

Autumn Days

The sea is calm, the skies are clear,
Can Christmas really be so near?
The brent geese fly, high in the sky,
I wonder why
They come the same time every year?

The lawns have had their final cut,
Yet there remains a final but . . .
If grass gets long, if grass grows on,
They'll be redone.
The garden shed cannot be shut!

The evenings are drawing in,
The hedges need their winter trim,
The beds all need a final weed
Or else the seed
Will bring the weeds all back in spring.

The central heating's been turned on,
Our bags of coal are not all gone,
There's quite a stack out at the back
And every sack
Will help to put the winter on.

The winter woollies must come out,
Cos that's what autumn's all about.
They're a tight fit and scratch a bit,
But stick with it
And they'll last till you 'cast a clout'!

Patrick Davies

THE FIRST OF FALL

It rained this day
the first of fall
the sun it did not shine
the wind was cool
under autumn's rule
the birds they flew away
today I kissed you all windswept
our hearts beat as one
under autumn skies
where our true love lies
rejoicing in the fall.

Margery Rayson

AUTUMN

Summer bounty's all around
Brown and crinkly on the ground
Autumn's here and winter soon
We've already seen the harvest moon

Summer bounty's all around
Blown by the wind, along the ground
Brown and crinkly, there they lay
In the ever shortening day

Soon the frost will nip one's ear
And the sun may give us cheer
Though our spirits may get higher
We'll have to huddle by the fire

Yes, this is autumn
When pear and plum
Ripen and fall
For the pleasure of us all.

Derek Spencer

Autumn

As you walk among the trees
Beautiful colours you see
The green of spring has turned to gold
And the sap is leaving the tree
Everything is slowing down
Now the summer's gone
Animals are going to ground
The birds have lost their song
The sheep are on the mangolds
The cows are in the byre
The farmer has his crops in
And rests beside the fire
This is the compensation
For losing the summer sun
But if you use your imagination
Autumn can be fun!

Jessie E Bishop

Autumn Returns

Autumn returns wearing a golden crown
and flowing multicoloured robes.
Her spirit flies free over the land
food for the body and soul of mankind.

The forest ablaze with vibrant colour
all shades of gold, red and brown
fruit and berries are plentiful
birds are busy taking their fill.

Cottage gardens a colourful picture
late flowers for the bees gathering nectar
the pathway is strewn with papery leaves
swirling and rustling swept forth in the breeze.

Summer visitors have departed
robins have started to sing again
the orchard abundant with scarlet fruit
mouth-watering, ready to eat.

Autumnal frost transforms the pool
silver, mystical and beautiful
dew laden cobwebs sparkle
a passing exquisite work of art.

Autumn returns wearing a golden crown
and flowing multicoloured robes
captured in the rosy light of dawn
her spirit flies free over the land.

Beth Izatt Anderson

WHERE SILVER SPIDER WEBS AND FROST COVERED BLACKBERRIES MEET, IS IT REALLY FANTASY OR WHERE TRUE ROMANCE TURNS ON ITS HEAT?

Looking across the late summer early morning misty scene;
The sunlight begins to trickle through the silver spider webs
Across the white early frost covered blackberries awakening dream.
I'm only nineteen summers old, yet all woman through and through:
The joyous majesty of such a late summer scene thrills me as I view.
Now I hear the magic melodies of the first birdsong
In the joyful chorus of early autumn season:
Already, summer seems to be vanishing in the glorious shades
Of autumn's splendour without any tinge of regretful reason.
I just love to see the horses and ponies at play:
I look for my own brave stallion the master of all he does survey.
Casting off my gown of night, ready to bathe in a caressing shower
Of morning's early exhilaration as I anticipate what's coming my way:
Oh so joyful at riding my favourite mount sharing happy pleasures
At the beginning of such a wonderful heart-pounding day.
When I will ride out naked into the fields of perfumed late summer
flowers; with the early morning sun warming my unadorned nude form
Passing away the sunny hours.
I jump up on my fearless stallion and he yields to the total woman: me!
For though I'm only nineteen summers old, I am nude,
                              proud and fearless:
No one controls my own destiny.
Now I am as one with the rampant charging mount between my thighs:
Riding through the last summer's wild flowers with ecstasy the prize.
I feel my brave stallion responding to the need for speed within me:
For I am really feeling lithe and lissom. Oh how I enjoy being a she.
Rising up and down as we ride faster and faster into the new sun:
I am now enjoying the first sweet moments of having total fun.
I am a queen of all I see, riding naked to meet my white knight
For I am unashamed of such imagination and urgent desire
Which is my womanly delight and right.

Such waves of wanton pleasure come over me as if I'm in a dream:
With sweet joy and ecstasy rippling and cascading over me
                                              like caressing sun rays,
I must not leave the wild passion of a last summer scene.
Suddenly my mount rises up too far, and I fall gasping to the ground:
I hear bells ringing all around me, and I cannot escape the sound.
Sadly then I return to morning reality,
As I awake naked, alone, in my own bed.
The living dream to which I so joyfully surrendered to
Was a sweet, romantic fantasy in my own head!
Yet still I hope that my sweet prince will wait for me: my royal sire:
As I ride naked to meet him to fulfil my urgent desire.
Now I can't wait to dream again of another last late summer dawn,
When I will again ride totally naked on my warm rampant stallion
To celebrate another golden early autumn young woman's love morn.

Jackie J Docherty

THE FOX'S POINT OF VIEW

The colours remind me autumn has arrived,
Reds, browns then the falling leaves,
A trail of crispness that worries me,
I have to be on my guard now.

Blackberries in abundance eases the
Gnawing hunger for just a little while,
Perhaps I'll catch a rabbit or hare,
To sustain me through the night.

The day grows cruel, a biting wind,
Trees sway and creek, reminding me,
Summer is going to sleep,
But for me my senses awaken.

Each day I live as my last,
A horn blows in the distance,
Why do they descend on me,
When my stomach is empty.

In my bury there's no solitude,
As the shovels above increase my senses,
Sounds are like thunder my heart drums louder,
As I make ready my escape.

But fool I am, there's no escape for me,
Glinting eyes, savage teeth, enter my domain,
No cunning trick can help me out
Of the death they are going to claim.

Jane Margaret Isaac

AUTUMN

Autumn brings with it colours of every hue,
Round each and every corner a different view.
Autumn's many shades of browns and golds,
Darker days and nights just waiting to unfold.

The trees in the woods so majestic and tall,
Seem to be sad as they watch leaves fall.
A carpet of colours so crunchy and new,
Gone are the flowers so beautiful, now so few.

Winter beckons and we think of days so dark,
Of gardens gone to sleep so dismal and stark.
We close curtains and doors making it cosy and warm,
Keeping us so snug away from the cold and storm.

But each new season brings a beauty all its own,
Autumn plants sleep, spring the seeds are sown.
We look for the rainbow after the rain,
It's for sure that no two days will ever be the same.

Barbara Ann Barker

A Time To Rest

Delicate lace, like gems they sparkle and shine,
These are the webs through the hedges entwine,
A white veil engulfs us, not making a sound,
No sunshine or brightness today will be found,
By nightfall she's gone, she just couldn't stay,
Her brother came calling and bid her away,
He's strong and he's loud, all know he is there,
He fights through the trees, and tousles our hair,
But Mother reminds them it's time now to rest,
For when spring calls, we must be at our best,
So the trees surrender, until naked and bare,
The blooms bright and proud, no longer they stare,
So shelters are made, resting places are dug,
In time for his visit, tucked up all snug,
White fluttering wings, he spreads over us all,
Just those prepared will escape his fall,
His time is short, Father never stays long,
When you wake in the morning he'll probably be gone,
So for now, we remain, red, gold and brown,
As Mother Earth wears, her autumnal crown.

Judy Taylor

AUTUMN'S MAGICAL MILE

There is magic in every autumn day,
Sometimes a stillness, or sunny or grey,
Always exciting, changeable and new.
Raindrops bring coloured brollies into view,
Sunny spells complete the scenery anew
Excitement arrives when there is a rainbow too!

Branches wave excitedly from the tall trees,
Autumn's red and gold leaves float away in the breeze,
Forming a rustling carpet with conkers here and there,
This is the fall when everything is laid bare.
When chilly winds arrive, wrap up, wear a smile,
Wear it and share it along autumn's magical mile.

. . . And for all who are privileged to see,
Give thanks! Remember some folks, are not so lucky!

S M Bush-Payne

ANCHOR BOOKS
SUBMISSIONS INVITED
SOMETHING FOR EVERYONE

ANCHOR BOOKS GEN - Any subject, light-hearted clean fun, nothing unprintable please.

THE OPPOSITE SEX - Have your say on the opposite gender. Do they drive you mad or can we co-exist in harmony?

THE NATURAL WORLD - Are we destroying the world around us? What should we do to preserve the beauty and the future of our planet - you decide!

All poems no longer than 30 lines.
Always welcome! No fee!
Plus cash prizes to be won!

Mark your envelope (eg *The Natural World*)
And send to:
Anchor Books
Remus House, Coltsfoot Drive
Peterborough, PE2 9JX

**OVER £10,000 IN POETRY PRIZES
TO BE WON!**

Send an SAE for details on our latest competition!